# Memoirs of a
# CAREGIVER

# Memoirs of a CAREGIVER

A Caregiver's Story of
Assisting Four Family
Members with
Alzheimer's Disease

## CYNTHIA YOUNG

iUniverse, Inc.
Bloomington

Memoirs of a Caregiver
A Caregiver's Story of Assisting Four Family
Members with Alzheimer's Disease

During the writing of this story, names and events may have been omitted or changed to protect the privacy of others.

For information, address Cynthia Young, 2276 Griffin Way, Suite 105-195; Corona, California 92879.

First paperback edition January 2013

For information about special discounts for bulk purchases, please contact Cynthia Young at 1-951-205-9810 or cyoungbooks@gmail.com.

iUniverse books may be ordered through booksellers or by contacting:

iUniverse
1663 Liberty Drive
Bloomington, IN 47403
www.iuniverse.com
1-800-Authors (1-800-288-4677)

Because of the dynamic nature of the Internet, any web addresses or links contained in this book may have changed since publication and may no longer be valid. The views expressed in this work are solely those of the author and do not necessarily reflect the views of the publisher, and the publisher hereby disclaims any responsibility for them.

ISBN: 978-1-4759-7101-9 (sc)
ISBN: 978-1-4759-7100-2 (hc)
ISBN: 978-1-4759-7099-9 (e)

Library of Congress Control Number: 2013900490

Printed in the United States of America

iUniverse rev. date: 01/28/2013

Dedicated to my mother, Alice

# Contents

# Acknowledgments

I have not been alone in my quest to accomplish the publishing of this book. Over the years, I have had many sources of inspiration; the ones that stand out far and above are my family members and friends.

My heartfelt appreciation goes out to my husband, Darryl, who walked this path with me and endured many long months of separation during this journey.

To my daughter, Tonia; my friends Winnye and Debbie; and my sister-in-law, Barbara—I thank them for their opinions, beat-downs, kicks in the butt, and pick-me-ups that made me laugh when I felt like crying. They supported me through hours of phone conversations and talked me through the tears, heartbreak, and depression I sometimes felt would overwhelm and consume me over these years. They have listened to my ideas, commiserated with me, encouraged me, and propelled me forward to the completion of this book.

And finally, I want to thank Krista Hill, my editorial consultant, for holding my hand and encouraging me to move forward when I was overwhelmed with the daunting task of writing this book.

# Caregivers' Elegy

Cynthia Young
March 2011

**Dedicated to Caregivers Everywhere**

I pray that I will always care for those I love with passion and grace,
but with all the caring comes responsibilities that are hard to face.

These twenty-four-hour days are something I don't want.
I'm not having any fun,
I'm tired, and it makes me sad
to see my loved one trying to hang on.

I feel like screaming, shouting, and crying out.
Sometimes it's hard to get my laughter out.

I just want you back the way you were,
remembering the good times from back in the day,
but there's a fork in the road taking us a different way.

No matter which way things go, you bring me joy.
Your wise childlike eyes make me know
that I'm really the one reaping the prize.

When I see your smile and innocence now,
I just want to love you, kiss you,
and do all I can to protect you.

God has the master plan,
and I know that angels are guiding me through
to do what He has put me here to do.

As I see to your needs, I can't forget about me.
I need to refresh to be a better me.
I'll follow God's master plan wherever it leads,
knowing that one day, we'll both be free.

# Introduction

Many of our nation's cities are plagued with killings, drug abuse, child and elder abuse, thefts, bullying, and much more.

But as horrendous as these things are in their nature, our aging population is being assaulted by yet another predator that steals them from their loved ones by taking their memory and independence and eventually whittling them away.

Alzheimer's disease is a progressive brain disorder that gradually destroys a person's memory and ability to learn, reason, make sound judgments, communicate, and carry out daily activities.

My mother's doctor explained to me that the brain begins to shrink as Alzheimer's progresses and will separate, causing fissures that disrupt normal functions. The doctor continued to explain that people with Alzheimer's die an average of eight years after first experiencing symptoms, but the duration of the disease can vary from three to twenty years.

As it progresses, a person may experience changes in personality and behavior, such as anxiety, suspiciousness, or agitation, as well as delusions and hallucinations. In its late stages, individuals may need assistance with dressing, personal hygiene, eating, and other basic functions.

It began for me in 2002 when I discovered that my eldest and youngest aunts had Alzheimer's. That discovery was just the beginning of my journey, and at that time I certainly didn't have a clue about what I didn't know. My wildest imagination could not prepare me for what I was about to undertake.

Looking back at my past to happier times, I can say that growing up in Detroit, Michigan, in the sixties was a blast. The sound of Motown was rampant in our city, and it was prosperous, beautiful, and vibrant in those days.

I am an only child who lived in a two-parent household until my mother and father divorced when I was twelve years old. I was devastated by their divorce. My dad continued to be there for me, and my mother's family and friends surrounded us with love and support. I never felt deprived of anything.

I became a teen mom, and once again my mom and dad and family supported my daughter and me. My parents encouraged me to pursue my education. I returned to Northwestern High School, graduated with high grades, and attained my high school diploma. I never attended college; instead, I went to work to support myself and my child. I have worked various jobs throughout my lifetime.

I am certainly not an expert in caregiving, but my experiences have heightened my ability to be a tenacious, extremely loving, patient, loyal, steadfast, compassionate, and fierce protector. These qualities have sustained me through the past ten years of my caregiving experiences, along with my family and friends' support.

Here is my story.

When I was a child, I remember my mother getting phone calls from my grandmother telling her to get everyone in the family over to her house. Mom, Dad, and I lived only four blocks away from her, and on occasion Mom (with me in tow) would rush to Grandmama's house to look for Granddaddy because he had wandered off again. My mother and aunts would spread out through the neighborhood looking for him. When they found him, he had no idea how he had gotten so far from home. I heard my family refer to him as being "senile."

I didn't find out until I was a grown woman that Granddaddy had been committed to a psychiatric hospital for this behavior that no one really understood. Aunt Helen's decision to commit him caused quite a rift in the family as not everyone agreed with her decision. And I don't know much more than that.

I had to face the fact that I didn't know or even remember a lot about my family history. Why? Because when my mother was trying to explain things to me—for instance, who this great-uncle was and who his children were or where the relatives in the South lived—I simply didn't want to hear about that; I was in the club and having fun. None of what she was talking about interested me, and I could not see the relevance of it then.

If I knew then what I know now, I would have held a tape recorder up to her mouth and listened intently to what she had to say. I am glad I didn't totally ignore everything she said. Some of it stuck, and I was grateful for what I did retain and the bits and pieces I picked up from documents. I learned later on that knowing more about the family history could unravel questions about how things got to be the way they are. It could answer questions about who died from what ailments and how those threads of history translate into what affects those still living.

Having just one family member become incapacitated with Alzheimer's is tragic and overwhelming. But I had to care for *four* loved ones afflicted with this memory-robbing, debilitating disease.

My hope in writing about my experiences is to help others like me become more empowered in this genre of caregivers. Whether you choose to speak to friends, support groups, or a professional therapist, be sure to talk to people about your situation; you never know who may be able to enlighten you with helpful information. Perhaps you will read my story and something about what I have been through and continue to go through will resonate with you. I hope that I will give you inspiration and encouragement to do what you feel you must do and, most importantly, what you want to do to help your loved one.

# Chapter One—Discover and Recover

## 2002

### Aunt Helen

Aunt Helen was a light-skinned, buxom redhead with a big personality (who reminded me of "Lucy") and a big pretty smile. She was a joyful person most of the time, but we all knew when she was serious about something and didn't want to play. Helen, nicknamed "Bootsie," was someone to be reckoned with and was a major player in her family of eight brothers and sisters (my maternal aunts and uncles). She was the fourth child of eight. Aunt Helen married young, and she and her husband seemed to be the ideal couple, at least from a child's perspective. They worked together and played together, but they did not have children together.

Some of my fondest childhood memories are of going to their house for Christmas. Aunt Helen loved everything that embodied Christmas and was like a kid in the candy store at Christmastime, putting up lots of lights and decorations and always having a gift for anyone who came through her door. She loved her candy, nuts, and pistachio ice cream—practically anything that was sweet—and you could always find dishes around the house filled with the cavity-building treats.

She was a jokester too! I remember a joke she pulled on her sisters. Auntie called her sisters one by one and said, "Girl, I just bought a four-carat ring!" The sisters were so excited that they rushed over to Aunt Helen's house to see the ring. For crying out loud, the ring had four miniature plastic carrots on it! My mother and her sisters were too outdone because they all fell for it; I can still hear Aunt Helen howling at them with laughter.

Just before Christmas 1973, as usual Auntie was struggling with her weight. I stopped by to see her, and she told me she started a new diet. "Penny [she always called me by my nickname], I started a new diet today."

"Really?" I asked. "What's the name of the diet?"

With a sly smile, she said, "The see-food diet."

"I've never heard of this diet, Auntie. How does it work?"

"All it entails is eating all the food you can see!"

That girl had jokes, didn't she? But Auntie had her share of tears too. On September 13, 1996, Auntie awakened to find that her beloved husband had passed away during the night. After his passing she never seemed to be the same. It was as though the joy and light had gone out of her life.

Years after her husband's death, Aunt Helen still talked about him and how much she missed him. Over time, she seemed to slowly lose interest in her church (which she loved dearly) and other outside activities. She stopped going out and became a recluse.

The first indication that something was wrong came in 2001. My daughter, Tonia, and I went to Detroit to see my mother receive an award from her alumni association at Cobo Hall. It was important to Mom to be surrounded by family members and friends, and we were there to support her that night. The day of the awards ceremony, Mom asked Tonia and me to go over to Auntie's house and bring her to the ceremony. When we arrived at the house, she was not ready.

"I'm not going," she told us.

"Auntie," I explained, "Mom's going to be very disappointed if you don't come. She's really looking forward to you being there."

Aunt Helen seemed confused and unsure of what was going on and what she should do. She refused to get in the bathtub, so we washed her up from the sink. I had never seen her like this and started to feel a sense of dread, but I couldn't put my finger on exactly why I felt that way.

While I was working on getting Auntie bathed, Tonia was scouring the closets for an outfit for her to wear (she had lost a lot of weight), and she came across a notebook. She also found a checkbook and uncashed checks in a dresser drawer. As soon as we finished getting Aunt Helen ready, we gathered up all the things Tonia had found and took them with us. A few days later, as I began to organize the items Tonia found in the closet and drawers, I discovered bills that had not been paid or were overpaid. Auntie had written checks in large amounts for household items, groceries, and bills, and to people she knew.

At times we all forget where we left our keys, or why we went into a room to do something and then could not remember what we were there for, or forget to make a bill payment. But the number of things that Auntie was not handling was more than forgetfulness. I knew that my aunt was a good businesswoman and was meticulous in taking care of her business. So for me this was a sign of another problem.

Playing devil's advocate, I will say that Auntie was a generous person, but in her right mind, I don't think she would have been as overly generous as the amounts on these checks indicated. I believe she was coerced into writing those checks. If that was the case, then it could be the reason my mother was kept at arm's length. My mother became suspicious that someone was influencing Auntie when she didn't get to talk to her, and she could never get inside the house when she stopped by to visit. These sisters talked practically every day, and now Auntie looked at Mom through the peephole in the door and told her she didn't want any company. No, something was going on; Aunt Helen and Mom were very close, too close for her to shut Mom out without an explanation.

Back in the day, neighbors were closer knit; people looked out for each other. Auntie lived in her neighborhood for fifty-plus years in a Tudor-style house with a well-manicured lawn, shrubs, and colorful flower beds. The block she lived on was quiet and lined with plenty of shade trees and more well-kept homes. She had long-lasting friendships with her neighbors; they knew our family and we knew theirs. Aunt Helen's neighbor across the street saw me outside one day and began to tell me that he had seen people go in to Aunt Helen's with nothing and come out with bags of stuff on more than one occasion. Now that I was aware of and seeing for myself what was going on, trust and believe that the gravy train was over for whoever was taking advantage of her!

I sat down with Aunt Helen and convinced her to let Mom take over paying the bills and buying the groceries. Mom resumed the routine of talking with her sister and checked on her by phone daily. Things seemed to be back on track for a while after Tonia and I returned home. A few months passed without incident. Then Mom received a disturbing call from the neighbors telling her that Auntie was in the middle of the street in the dead of winter, taking in trash cans in her nightclothes.

On another occasion, one of the neighbors went to visit and smelled gas throughout the house. My mother would find half-eaten microwave dinners in the oven. With all these incidents piling up, Mom decided that she needed to do something. In February 2002, she called me at work to tell me that she had to bring her sister to her house because she was afraid for her safety. Aunt Helen wasn't having it; she cursed at my mom and tried to leave. Mom had to remove the key from the front door to keep her from walking away. As the months progressed, Auntie got worse and began talking out loud to her father and other deceased family members. This terrified my mother, who herself admits to being scared of dead people.

I received another call in June from Mom telling me that things were worse with Auntie and that she was afraid of her. She asked for my help. I requested two weeks off from work and went to Detroit in July. Mom was right—something needed to be done for Aunt Helen. I could see that she needed professional help. I noticed that she could not hold a conversation with me; her state of mind seemed confused. She talked out loud to herself constantly, and that, along with other things I had seen, made me sure that we needed to take her to see someone. When I suggested this to my mother, she jumped to the conclusion that I was talking about a nursing home. She said, "There is no way I am taking my sister to a nursing home; my father told us to stick together." I was able to get her to agree that we should at least take Auntie to the doctor for a checkup. The doctor stated that Aunt Helen had Alzheimer's disease and suggested that she should be in a nursing home.

After talking with the doctor and assessing the situation, I sat down with Mom to tell her the way I saw things, that Aunt Helen required more care than she could provide. She didn't seem to understand what was happening to her sister. Since she had already put her foot down about a nursing home, she enlisted her friends to watch Aunt Helen while she went to work. My mother had officially retired from her job with the Detroit Board of Education years before but continued to work on a part-time basis.

Having spoken to Mom over the phone and hearing her description of Auntie's behavior and having seen things for myself in 2001, I was convinced this behavior was no longer something we could ignore, and with confirmation from the doctor, I couldn't let Mom live in a bubble trying to pretend it wasn't happening.

I began to research Alzheimer's disease on the computer, searching the Internet using the word "Alzheimer's". I went to the Alzheimer's Association website for information and obtained a wealth of information on the disease. The US Department of Health and Human Services, National Institute on Aging, and the National Institute of Health also offered publications for caregivers.

With all the research I had done, I tried to explain Alzheimer's to my mother. I suggested that we take classes and read up on it to know what to expect and how to handle the different behaviors (besides the ones we already had experienced) that Auntie would eventually start to exhibit. Mom didn't want to hear any of it; she seemed to me to be very unreasonable and I guess even in denial. Since she wasn't listening or hearing what I had to say, I recruited Tonia, thinking that Mom would listen to her if not to me. When Tonia arrived in town, we sat Mom down and tried to come up with a plan that would allow her to continue working and keep Auntie at home.

We finally suggested that we should look into an adult day-care program; that would give Mom the freedom to continue her part-time job and give Auntie an outing each day. By the time Auntie returned home in the evening, Mom would be back from work and they could have dinner, watch TV, and retire to bed. She reluctantly agreed. With a little leeway, Tonia and I began to scour the city for day-care facilities for Aunt Helen. But little did we know that things were about to hit the fan once again!

## Aunt Margaret

Aunt Margaret is the youngest of Mom's siblings. She and I shared the sign of Leo; her birthday was the day before mine. She always called me her baby. While my mom and dad were saving their money to buy a house for us, I lived at my grandparents' house, and Aunt Margaret lived there too. She would babysit me sometimes.

I remember how beautiful her light brown skin was and how radiant her complexion looked. She had beautiful hands with long, tapered fingers and pretty feet, and she always kept her nails polished. Mom told me that Auntie loved playing the piano and that their parents opted to buy Margaret a piano rather than use the money to send my mother to college. It seems that after that, my mom harbored some resentment. I was told that everyone seemed to boss Auntie around like she was still a child (especially Aunt Helen) and that she resented it. After time passed, she moved away from Grandmama's house and became the elusive butterfly, so to speak. She pretty much stayed away from the family and only came around occasionally. She had a temper and could become volatile quickly.

I was about eleven years old when I personally experienced her mean streak. One day while babysitting, she began to taunt me by telling me that I wasn't going to have a mother and father anymore because my parents were splitting up! I yelled at her that she didn't know what she was talking about and started to run away from her. I could hear her taunting me by calling me an orphan. Needless to say, my mother was furious when she found out about this, and heated words were exchanged between them.

Even when there is dissension within a family, they will stick together when it counts. In 2002, my mother stepped up to help her sister. Aunt Margaret never married and had no children. For more than twenty years, she lived alone in an apartment on Detroit's east side. Mom was listed with the apartment management as an emergency contact, so they contacted my mother when Auntie didn't pay her rent and was about to be evicted. Years before, when Auntie still worked at the hospital, she took Mom and me to her credit union and added us to her account as signatories. This would prove to be a blessing years later. Mom took care of the arrearage, because Aunt Margaret was not acting rationally. She told Mom she had paid the rent and the manager was lying when clearly that wasn't the truth.

While out searching for day-care facilities one day, Tonia and I stopped to eat at a fast-food restaurant. I decided to check in with Mom to see how things were going at the house. When Mom answered the phone, she was hysterical, telling me, "Cyn, Margaret's apartment building manager called and told me that Margaret was seen by her neighbors on her floor running naked in the hallway!"

What! I couldn't believe what I was hearing. Tonia and I headed for her apartment to see for ourselves what was going on. When we arrived, the manager told us that Aunt Margaret had gone to her apartment. She also mentioned that another resident had taken an interest in Auntie and was helping her out.

She said the lady lived on the fifth floor and her name was Ms. Russell. First, we went to Aunt Margaret's apartment on the eleventh floor and knocked on the door. Aunt Margaret answered and let us in. (She was fully clothed.) Once we went in, I was dumbfounded and was in no way prepared for what I saw there. On the heels of our recent discovery that Aunt Helen had Alzheimer's and all that could entail, what I saw in Aunt Margaret's apartment was undeniably a display of the same symptoms and more!

All my aunts kept immaculate homes, and what I saw was a bizarre scene from someone else's life; this couldn't be happening to someone in my family. But it was; here we were right in the middle of a nightmare. Newspapers, Styrofoam takeout boxes, clothes, and feces covered the floors in the entryway and living room. The bed was unmade and smelled of urine, the mattress had rotted, and the bathtub was filled with clothes. There was no food in the refrigerator or cabinets, and sticky notes and address labels covered the refrigerator with her name, address, and phone number on them. It seemed that she had written notes to remind herself who she was and where she lived because she was forgetting these things.

The family had always said that Margaret was schizophrenic, and she had demonstrated those symptoms and behaviors in the past, but what we saw was not that—it clearly was Alzheimer's. Nevertheless, Auntie was cheerful and glad to see us and seemed very much unfazed by her surroundings. We eventually went to see Ms. Russell, and she quickly brought us up to date. She informed us that Auntie knocked on her door one day and asked her for something to eat, and since that day she had been feeding her and checking on her daily.

Auntie seemed to trust her and got along well with her. Ms. Russell said that they often saw each other in the apartment-complex community center for social events and had become friendly. I reimbursed Ms. Russell for the food she had already given our aunt, and she agreed to continue caring for her. We agreed on a monthly payment for her services, and I gave her money for the groceries. The next day, we returned and began cleaning up Aunt Margaret's apartment.

With a plan in place for Aunt Margaret, we resumed our search for and finally found a day-care facility for Aunt Helen to attend. It was the best facility in Detroit out of the many we visited. After visiting five other facilities, we felt that this one was different from the moment we walked in. The doors were securely locked (to prevent someone from walking away from the facility), the main room was bright and cheerful, and the clients were being engaged by the staff and seemed to be enjoying themselves playing games that enhanced memory. Music (that seniors would relate to) played softly in the background. Extra services were also available for their hair and nails, and what impressed me the most was the full-service kitchen that served hot meals daily. Transportation was provided if needed, and the owners were hands-on with their business. So a couple of weeks later, after completing paperwork and physical examinations, Aunt Helen began day care at the Senior Activity Center (SAC) Adult Day Care Inc., in Detroit.

As the ultimate decision maker, my mother was kept in the loop on all that needed to be done, but she didn't seem to have any interest. She just wanted to go to her job. The next thing I knew,

Tonia and I were in the midst of updating Aunt Helen's house so it could be rented to defray the cost of the day-care expenses. We also had to finish the cleanup and replace flooring at Aunt Margaret's apartment. With all of this going on, my mother decided that she was being neglected and no one was paying any attention to her (the victim). She became antagonistic and complained about everything. I was updating her daily on our progress and asking for her consent to move forward on things that needed to get started when she told me that her house needed work too! To appease her, I agreed to decorate her house too, and we discussed what she'd like done.

While searching for tradesmen and carpet to get these updates done, I called a young salesman named Paul who had advertised in the yellow pages. After talking with him, I was very much impressed. He owned his own flooring business and was well connected around town with tradesmen because he was into flipping houses. I invited him to bring his flooring samples to Mom's house, and he convinced me that he was the man for the job.

During our meeting, Tonia came in to the room, and it was like watching one of those commercials where two people are running toward each other in slow motion. After he laid eyes on my beautiful daughter, I don't think Paul heard a word I was saying. Once he recovered and began to focus on the subject at hand, Tonia and I explained the scope of work that needed to be done. He couldn't believe how much we were undertaking. Knowing that we were on a short time frame and had to return to work soon, he said he would help us source tradesmen to do the work needed. Needless to say, I hired him to do the flooring for all three projects. Paul had an infectious smile and was really down to earth. It felt like we had known him forever. Mom and Aunt Helen took to him right away, and from that point on he was like family.

The next day, we met Paul at his store to pick out flooring, and we all decided to hook up that evening. He picked us up, and we proceeded to the club. I had the best night dancing that I had had in many, many, many years. He was right, I needed to get rid of a lot of stress, and dancing the night away was a good way to do it.

Upon looking at Aunt Helen's assets, we told Mom that she should see an attorney and both of them should have a power of attorney or will written up. We met with the attorney a few days later, and Mom made out her power of attorney and will. But because Aunt Helen could not handle her own business, she was considered an incapacitated individual. We were advised by the attorney that Mom should petition the probate court to become Aunt Helen's court-appointed guardian and conservator. Becoming a court-appointed guardian gave her the authority to make decisions on Aunt Helen's behalf (like where she lives, medical decisions, etc.). As court-appointed conservator, Mom had the authority to make decisions regarding Aunt Helen's finances and assets (bank accounts, real property, etc.).

The real work began by going through Aunt Helen's house and purging more than fifty years' worth of paperwork and her belongings. I held garage sales three weeks in a row, and it really hurt me to get rid of Auntie's belongings. Selling her things tore through me like a hot poker. The thought of anyone but her living there made me cry; at times I felt I couldn't do it. I thanked God for Tonia, my friend Winnye, and my in-laws, who helped me out big-time.

While work was going on at Aunt Helen's, the worked progressed at Mom's and Aunt Margaret's. At Aunt Margaret's we had to make it livable again by removing the trash buildup, putting her clothes back in the closets, replacing carpet, and buying a new mattress set.

One day, while Tonia and Paul were at Aunt Margaret's preparing the house for the carpet installers, my brother-in-law Wallace and I went back to the store to exchange the bed frame I had purchased for Aunt Margaret's bed.

We were on Van Dyke waiting at the light. When the light turned green and I proceeded to cross Gratiot, another car (an older-model Lincoln Town Car, built like a tank) hit the front end of the new Lincoln Town Car (built with lots of plastic) I was driving and spun us around, landing us back against the curb; during this spinning, my head was bouncing off the window. I was dazed and could only think about Tonia. I had the presence of mind to call and let her know where we were and what happened moments before I blacked out. Wallace was unharmed.

As the paramedics started to drive away, I could hear pounding on the back doors of the ambulance; it was Tonia screaming at them to stop. I was taken to the hospital and diagnosed with a concussion. Later that night, I was told that Tonia had driven past the backed-up traffic on Van Dyke on the sidewalk to get to the intersection. I was also told that the woman driving the other car had no insurance and tried to flee the scene but was apprehended by witnesses at the bus stop. We also found out later that she had struck my car so hard that the tie rod was completely severed.

After the accident, I turned my attention back to my mother, who, by the way, still had not attended a class or read anything about Alzheimer's so she would know what to expect and how to handle it. And with Aunt Margaret's condition looking very similar, there was no doubt we needed to go. I took matters into my own hands and researched and found a class for us to attend (by contacting my local Alzheimer's Association) on the east side of Detroit. The day we were scheduled to go to class, I was in the living room when my mother entered the room.

I asked her, "Mom, are you ready for the class this afternoon?"

She turned and screamed at me, "I can't take this anymore!" and bolted down the stairs and ran down the street, leaving me standing in the middle of the living room wondering what I had just witnessed.

Is that what a nervous breakdown looks like? I didn't know. My head hurt from the accident, and since I had at this point been away from work a month, I was also now on the phone with my boss, answering questions about open issues that needed to be resolved. My plate was overflowing! And I really missed my husband and home. Nevertheless, things had to get done, and I couldn't stop now.

Mom returned home late that evening and never apologized for leaving the way she did. I told her, "Momma, you're not going to get away with what you did this morning. I rescheduled the class, and you had better not pull that mess again. I am working my ass off to help you, but you also have to help yourself." I continued to explain, "These are your sisters, not mine. I'm only obligated to take care of you!" That seemed to wake her up, and we attended the next class without incident.

But when we got to class, she was very blasé and was not paying attention. When the teacher gave us a break, Mom saw one of the department heads from her job whom she admired who was also attending the class. While Mom was in the bathroom, I took the opportunity to enlist help from the department head. She told Mom how important it was to learn about this disease, and that seemed to straighten her right up. Man, what a stroke of luck it was to run into her that day, because that did the trick. Mom was on her best behavior during the rest of the class.

Now I have to say that reading about situations that may come up and how to handle them doesn't mean that you'll actually be able to handle them. Book scenarios are just that, and trying to follow them step by step according to the book may not always work. Keep in mind that the book should be used as a guideline; your situation may not go according to the book and will require you to use common sense, improvise, and think quickly on your feet to find a solution that works for you and your circumstances. For instance, Aunt Helen had to get up each morning to catch the van that picks her up for day care. However, she didn't want to get up, and when she said no, Mom didn't make her. She would just walk away. So in the interim Tonia and I would get Auntie up and get her bathed, fed, and dressed before the van came. The question still lingered—how would Mom handle it when we were not there?

Six weeks after I arrived, I finally had a paying tenant for Aunt Helen's house. I was fortunate to get someone through an insurance company that was temporarily housing a family in a hotel after their home burned to the ground. After the tenants moved in, I also hired one of Aunt Helen's former neighbors to be the property manager. He collected the rent and conducted periodic home inspections to make sure the house wasn't being destroyed.

With Aunt Helen's house generating income, Aunt Margaret living comfortably in her newly decorated apartment, and Mom's house practically finished except for the window treatments being installed, I left Detroit with a heavy but thankful heart, knowing that I did what I could to help them. I never forgot how my family stuck together and supported me when I was a rebellious teenager and teen mom. They didn't judge me; they rallied around me and my baby and took care of us. Now the time had come for me to do something for them.

I returned home to my loving and supportive husband, who knows about family. Like my mother, he is also the seventh child (of ten). Mom always considered that a special bond between them. When I returned home, he decided that it was about time for us to leave our town house and find a bigger house. We began our house search in September 2002, quickly found a house, and moved in three days before Christmas. As much as I love the holiday season, there was no way I felt like decorating for Christmas that year. I was just too tired. But we weren't too tired to celebrate our new home and ring in the New Year!

## 2003

I was constantly checking in with Mom to see how things were going with her getting Aunt Helen up for day care, and she assured me that everything was fine. But I found out later that as the weather got progressively worse she did not get Auntie up and day care was over. During one of our phone calls, Mom told me, "Cyn, Helen has become more agitated. She's talking nonstop, and nothing is making any sense. She's talking to Daddy like he's in the room with us, and it is really freaking me out." She also said that Auntie walked through the house at night not knowing where she was and frightened her to the point that she began locking her bedroom door at night to keep her out. Mom told me, "I was in the kitchen cooking dinner, and Helen walked up on me and hit me on my head and started to fight me. She's getting worse; something has to be done."

Alzheimer's distorts a person's personality. Aunt Helen was an alpha female who took charge and dared you to oppose her. This kind of take-no-prisoner attitude caused conflict in the family, but few bucked her. Because Mom was her younger sister, she was used to acquiescing. At times, this disease made Auntie even more aggressive.

Alzheimer's symptoms:

Mild: memory loss, confusion, trouble handling money and paying bills, poor judgment leading to bad decisions, mood swings, personality changes, and increased anxiety and/or aggression

Moderate: increasing memory loss and confusion, shortened attention span, problems recognizing friends and family, difficulty reading and writing, difficulty organizing thoughts and thinking logically, wandering, restlessness, agitation, anxiety, repetitive statements, movements, suspiciousness, paranoia, vulgar language, inability to carry out getting dressed

Severe: cannot recognize family or friends or communicate in any way, completely dependent on others for care, weight loss, seizures, skin infections, difficulty swallowing, groaning, moaning, increased sleeplessness, lack of bladder or bowel control

Depending on personal circumstances, any of these stages that loved ones are displaying may make caring for them on your own too much to handle. Seek assistance from a doctor, hospital social worker, or a caregivers' support group.

# Alice

In February 2003, Mom called me at work to tell me she had been to her doctor and had been diagnosed with a brain aneurysm. This news rocked my world! I couldn't catch my breath, and I wanted to scream out loud. I began to shake, my mind was scrambled, and I don't think I heard much more after that. After I composed myself, I called Tonia and informed her of what Mom said. We agreed that we needed to talk with her doctor and called him on a three-way to get more information. From what he told us, we determined that we needed to get to Detroit as soon as possible.

Tonia and I arrived in Detroit in March to attend an appointment Mom had with the neurosurgeon who was going to perform her aneurysm surgery. The doctor told us that the first doctor we spoke to had misinformed us; this appointment was the first time he had reviewed her CAT scans and met with her, and the actual surgery would be scheduled in the next few months. After we met with the surgeon, Tonia and I sat down with Mom and had another serious talk with her about Aunt Helen. With this new turn of events, it was apparent to all of us that she surely would not be able to care for her now. We proposed that we start searching for an assisted-living facility for her; this time Mom didn't put up a fight.

I consoled my mother and told her, "Momma, Granddaddy would be proud of what you have done for your sisters. Honey, you have nothing to be ashamed of, and by letting Auntie go to an assisted-living home, she's going to get the care she needs by trained professionals. It will be better for both of you, because you can be her sister again and not the caregiver."

Tonia and I went in search of assisted-living facilities and, like looking for day care, we checked out everything from the front door to the rooms, the overall facility, and the demeanor of the staff. We asked to see their certificates from their fire inspections and health inspections, etc. Tonia and I make a good team. We double-teamed the facility managers: Tonia asked questions that the layperson might not know to ask, such as whether their facility specialized in caring for Alzheimer's patients, were the fire certificates up to date (she asked to see them; we didn't just take their word for it!), and what kind of training the staff received and how often they were updated on the latest methods of caregiving. *Are they bonded, and has a criminal background check been done on each one of them? What kind of activities do you provide? How is the laundry done—individually or in a common load?* And for God's sake, if we smelled urine at the front door or anywhere else on our tour, we got the hell out and kept looking!

In April, we finally settled on a beautiful place with nice green belts of grass throughout the facility and an immaculate residential area. It was costly, but it was the best we could find. I bought some furniture to make Auntie's room homey and got her settled.

The tenants had moved from Auntie's house in March; to protect the house, I kept the property manager and my brother-in-law Wallace on to watch out for it as they had while the tenants were living there.

After I returned to California, the surgical nurse finally called and told me the surgery was scheduled for May. I returned to Detroit for the outpatient surgery. Mom's very good friend, Lily, and Wallace waited with me while Mom went into surgery. For some reason, I was calm and not at all nervous about her going into surgery, probably because I had the utmost confidence in her surgeon. The surgery was successful; the aneurysm was deflated and a stent inserted in Mom's neck for better blood flow. She went home the same day. *My mother is extremely resilient*, I thought. I was amazed at how much of a trooper she was after the surgery; it was as though nothing had happened and she was her effervescent self again.

I really don't know why I was surprised, as over the years she'd survived a divorce and cleaning toilets at the YWCA, she finished business school, got hired at the Detroit Public Schools Board of Education in the nonteaching personnel department, helped many people get jobs with the Board of Education, raised a wayward teenage daughter (that would be me), purchased her very first car before she learned how to drive, paid for her house, and kept her credit in stellar condition. When I looked back on all that she accomplished, I realized that she was the best role model I could have had in my life.

My mom had curves and beautiful skin the color of brown sugar, and a gap in her front teeth accentuated her smile. She loved music and was a good dancer and a good cook, and her pies and cakes were well known among family, friends, and coworkers. Mom was a hard worker and a loving and supportive mother. She was conscientious and fiercely loyal to her family, especially to her sister Helen.

Mom was appointed by the court to be Aunt Helen's guardian and conservator the previous September. As a conservator, Mom had to account for every penny spent from Aunt Helen's bank account. A few days after Mom's surgery, I set up a home office for her complete with a desk, file cabinet, and color-coded files for Aunt Helen, Aunt Margaret, and herself so she could keep all of their mail, bills, and receipts straight. She was required to do a fiduciary report annually and submit it to the court for review. I showed her how to do a simple spreadsheet to keep things in order. But she insisted on spending her money for Aunt Helen's bills and necessities when she should have been using Aunt Helen's money and recording what she spent on the spreadsheet.

After that was done and I could see that Mom was back to her normal routine without consequences, I returned to California and could barely concentrate on my work because of all that had happened in Detroit. Having a stressful job didn't help matters, believe me. But each day when I arrived at work I'd go to my office, close the door, and call Detroit to talk to the doctors, attorneys, caregivers, and family and friends who assisted Mom in my absence.

By June, Aunt Helen's savings had dwindled significantly. Assisted-living facilities are not inexpensive. In addition to the base rent, there are also levels of care that they charge for (for example, to administer one through six medications three times a day would cost $300 a month, but if another prescription is added and it's now seven pills, the costs just jumped to the next level, $600 a month—a $300 increase!). Add the sanitary products (disposable diapers, bed pads, etc.) and it's another category and more money. Laundry fees apply too; if Auntie didn't know how to get to the dining room for meals and required the service of someone to assist her that assistance would also cost extra. If they needed to take a meal to her room, they charged for that too.

With all the extras added to the base rent it wasn't long before we had to sell her house. That was an emotional roller-coaster ride all over again for me. I struggled to hold on to all my memories of those fun Christmas parties with my family. I did not want to sell that house! However, I would do what was necessary to keep her safe and well taken care of. With the sale of the house she was set for a while longer. Before that was gone, I would have to figure out what to do next.

A representative at the assisted-living home told me on the down low that their facility was required to have so many beds set aside in their skilled-nursing section for low-income residents. I knew that eventually I would need to get Aunt Helen a bed over there and that timing would be critical.

Before I could put her in a skilled-nursing facility and receive aid from the government, she had to be destitute. I had to sell off all of her assets (home—in some cases this may not apply—car, etc.) and do what is called a "spend down" of her bank accounts. Over all she could not have more than $2,000 to her name. Medicaid and Medicare have strict guidelines; you should consult with an agency or social worker for more detailed information on these government agencies' guidelines.

Prior to Mom's surgery, she had applied for and was appointed conservator/guardian for Aunt Helen. She was having difficulty handling that responsibility, even with the filing system I set up for her and the spreadsheet I had showed her how to use. She would constantly mail paperwork to me asking me what it was and what to do with it. I was feeling like I was going to be more involved than I wanted to be, and I was left with a sinking feeling that something wasn't right.

I decided to alleviate some of the responsibility that Mom had on her shoulders. Tonia and I discussed what we could do to help Mom. I applied for guardianship for Aunt Margaret, but the court turned me down, stating that I was not approved because I lived out of state. However, when Tonia applied, they granted it to her (and she lives where?—out of state!). It was the same judge, different day, and different outcome. Go figure! So Tonia helped me out by becoming the guardian for Aunt Margaret (on paper only). I now made the decisions on her behalf and paid her bills to help Mom out. I thought doing that would make it easier for Mom to handle Aunt Helen's paperwork and her own business.

In August the first fiduciary report was due in a month and the attorney was calling me to find out where it was. I finally had to step in and take it over to get it done. Oh my God, I walked into a hornet's nest. Mom didn't have receipts, checks were written from multiple checkbooks, and monies were taken from her bank account and not Aunt Helen's. It was a huge mess, and needless to say it did not balance. The attorney got the judge to go ahead and approve it based on Mom's age and lack of detailed accounting. From that point on I had to do what I could to take it over. What a nightmare; trying to go behind someone else and make things right was not easy. I became the ghost writer and did the report with Mom's name on it and we kept moving forward.

In September, Darryl booked a trip for us to go to Hawaii. Oh, yes, I really needed a break. When we stepped off the plane, it was raining cats and dogs; needless to say, we were not off to a good start on this vacation. By the evening, the downpour had subsided but it was still sprinkling. We didn't care; we went out to explore. It was his first time there, but I had been there in 1998 and had ideas on where we could go. We spent time with his family, who live there, and then we were off to the submarine ride, dinner on a ship, and more sightseeing. We enjoyed ourselves immensely.

In spite of me thinking that things might fall apart if I went on this trip, they didn't! Caregivers have to remember to take care of themselves first. But we don't always, and more of us die before the person we are taking care of because we don't. I like to use the airlines' analogy. They tell you that when the oxygen masks falls from the ceiling, put your mask on first and then help someone else.

By now it was late October and Aunt Margaret was doing well staying in her apartment with Ms. Russell seeing to her needs. But one day Ms. Russell said that Aunt Margaret became agitated and threatened her with a knife while she was trying to administer her medication. Ms. Russell said that she immediately left the apartment and called the police and paramedics. They transported Auntie to the hospital across the street from where she lived. Ms. Russell contacted me at work to explain what had transpired. I immediately called to check on Auntie to find out what her status was and was told that she was not there. Whaaaat! Where was she? I was told that she must have checked herself out. I could not believe these people. Nobody really seemed to know anything or give a damn!

My husband Darryl was in Detroit when this happened, and he and Ms. Russell went on a city-wide search looking for her. After searching homeless shelters and hospitals, they located Auntie at another hospital farther out on the east side in a psych ward. When Darryl approached her, she knew who he was and was joking and laughing with him like nothing was wrong. A few weeks later, the hospital transferred Auntie to a nursing home recommended to me by Ms. Russell. Ms. Russell visited daily at different times of the day, sometimes during the first shift and sometimes during the second shift, to make sure that the staff at the nursing home knew that they were being monitored and that Aunt Margaret had someone looking in on her.

There are many people in nursing homes who have no one to look in on them. They are virtually alone, and the only people they see daily are their caregivers. In reality, there are good and bad caregivers; when there is no one to monitor what is being done to someone who has no one, it really does leave the door open for possible abuse. Ms. Russell was well aware of what happens in nursing homes, and she took precautions to ensure that it did not happen to Aunt Margaret; I was grateful to her for that. Even with constant random monitoring, realistically, if there are bad people in the home, five minutes after you leave they could do something. On each visit, checking them over from head to toe, looking for cuts, bruises, sores, etc., may keep the staff alert to give the best possible care to your loved ones.

Shortly after the incident with Aunt Margaret, it was becoming increasingly clear to me that my mother was not the same. With this revelation, my heart sank to my feet. I didn't want to believe that she too was falling victim to the same fate as my aunts. I wanted to ignore the signs, but sooner or later I knew I would need to face the reality that she really was traveling the same path. Incredible!

After all the stuff that had been going on all year, some much-needed relief and frivolity was needed. My favorite time of the year was approaching, and Darryl and I were preparing to celebrate our second Christmas in our home. Winnye, who is one of my staunch supporters, came to California for a visit. Darryl and I decorated the house and put up a huge Christmas tree. Winnye is so much fun to be with; we laughed and giggled like schoolgirls.

Every morning, she would have her coffee and watch the sun rise over the mountains from my kitchen window. The most hilarious thing is that every evening like clockwork she would run upstairs to her room and wait for the eight-foot-tall Frosty the Snowman on our lawn to inflate. It was like watching a kid on Christmas morning. Eventually Winnye returned to Detroit, and Darryl and I celebrated

New Year's Eve with champagne and thoughts of the positive things the New Year could bring.

## 2004

After the holidays, I returned to work in January feeling refreshed. I left for Detroit in March to further assess the situation there and to dismantle Aunt Margaret's apartment.

She'd been in the nursing home five months now, and it was very apparent to me that she would not return to her home of more than twenty years. This was becoming a habit I didn't want to get into, but I had no choice.

I had to dispose of her belongings, and just like it was with Aunt Helen, giving away Aunt Margaret's belongings was hard for me. I remember that my mood was somber on that very dreary, cold, and rainy day. Winnye and I packed boxes and distributed her things to those who needed them. Because Ms. Russell had been such a good friend and caregiver, I gave her most of the household items for her grandson and his family.

I felt like another part of my history was being destroyed. It's an awful feeling to have to dispose of someone's life, whether it is encompassed in a tiny apartment or a big house. It almost makes it seem that you are dismissing what was once important in their life. I was distraught when I left for home in April. Thank God for work, because I am sure my depression would have been deeper if I had no outlet for it. No matter how tough I thought I was, no matter how I thought I could ward off the feelings of despair, it engulfed me, and I really didn't recognize it until I read about it.

I wasn't sleeping at night, I constantly had reruns of what happened during the day, and I was consumed with things that had to be done and how to do them from California. I woke up tired, feeling like my brain was in a fog. I ate everything in sight and my weight spiraled out of control, fueling my depression even more. Tears were spontaneous and sometimes uncontrollable. My PMS didn't help matters—I was a hot mess!

It dawned on me one day that I should get back to what had always worked for me in the past—exercising. I joined Weight Watchers, changed my eating habits, went to my masseuse once a week, and exercised almost daily. My outlook improved tremendously, and as the weight dropped off, I felt even better. I was handling work, home, and Detroit. But, frankly, I had to admit that I was overwhelmed. Even though I admitted that I was overwhelmed, I was in too deep to do anything but keep going the way I was. The things I was responsible for could not be delegated to anyone else. I just kept in mind there would be light at the end of the tunnel and one day I would not have my golden girls. So I sucked it up and kept moving.

Even when I was not in Detroit, I always had something to do for Mom or the aunties, like calling doctors, lawyers, and the nursing home and assisted-living home to check on Aunt Margaret and Aunt Helen. Sometimes it was hard for me to concentrate on what my employer was paying me to do for them. I also felt the need to call my mom almost daily. She had given up her part-time job after having her surgery, and without Aunt Helen there to care for, all she did now was sit around the house working on her "projects."

When Mom had told me about her decision to retire years before, I advised her to make sure she had a plan for retirement—traveling, part-time work, volunteering, etc.—and she did love working in her old department after she retired, before she brought Aunt Helen to the house to live with her. Now when I talked to her, she seemed to be slowing down, but she still kept herself busy around the house.

At seventy-six Mom was still cooking her meals and handling her household, just like always. She was still driving her car too. However, one day I got a call from her telling me that she'd been in an accident at a busy intersection not far from her house. Apparently, the light was green but Mom paused before making a right turn and a guy in a truck behind her hit her car. The crash drew some people out on their porches to see what happened. Mom told me that the man who hit her was seriously angry and was in her face yelling at her, so much so that he frightened her. Mom then ran up on a porch where two men were and asked to use their phone to call the police.

I was mortified when she told me that. I asked her where her cell phone was, and she informed me that she had given it back to the phone company months before and never mentioned it to me. I chastised her about not thinking and going into a house with two men she didn't know.

She fired back, "Listen here, Cynthia. I'm grown, and I've been living a lot longer than you have. I trust my instincts, and I could tell they were good people." I thought I would explode. This is Detroit, people, and it damn sure ain't what it used to be back in the fabulous fifties. The guy who hit her had pulled off by the time the police arrived. No big surprise there.

I spoke to Mom's friend Lily all the time. Mom and Lily had been friends since Mom got her a job in one of the schools. On one occasion we talked about the disturbing phone calls she was receiving from

Mom in the middle of the night. She said that Mom called one night and told her that she didn't know what time it was or where she was and that she was afraid that something was happening to her and she didn't know what it was. Lily said she comforted her that night and that the next day Mom had no recollection of the conversation. She only lived a few minutes from Mom, and she began to go over to Mom's house and spend time with her and would accompany her to doctor appointments and other places she had to go. My heart was sinking again; it was feeling more and more like déjà vu.

During all of this, I was blessed with an angel named Wallace. When I told Wallace what was happening with Mom, he stepped to the plate to help her out in my absence and had been helping out periodically since 2002. But now he was more involved. He would take Mom and Lily to the grocery store, on outings, and to doctor's appointments and would do other errands and odd jobs for them and just hang out with them. They loved him because he never made them feel they had to hurry and finish what they needed to do. In turn, they helped a brother out while he was in between jobs. So it was a beneficial relationship all around.

I had managed to spend down Aunt Helen's accounts over the past months, and I had just enough money to pay for one more month's rent on the assisted-living side of their facility and was under pressure to get her into the skilled-nursing unit before rent was due again. An opening came up right when we needed it, and she was fortunate to get a bed; my relief was palpable. She was transferred to the skilled-nursing unit of the assisted-living home in October.

I just finished booking my trip to Detroit in October when Wallace called one day to say that he had taken Mom to visit Aunt Helen and he and Mom were concerned because Auntie was lethargic and seemed very confused and wasn't talking. She had a bruise on her hand. A few days later, my cousin Teryl also went to see her and saw the bruise.

Teryl spoke with the nurses, and no one seemed to know a damn thing about it. She tried talking to a social worker, but the woman kept her waiting. When Teryl tried again to speak to her, she threw her hand up in Teryl's face and rudely told her she had to make a phone call and she would get to her in a minute!

When Teryl called to tell me about this incident and how rude this woman was, I was livid, because this was the same woman who had tried talking down to me when I was trying to get Aunt Helen moved from the assisted-living side of the facility to the skilled-nursing unit. I finally got through to a head nurse and was told that Auntie had fallen from the bed and had a hair-line fracture and a small bump on her head. We should have been informed as soon as it happened, but we weren't, and so I was angry. Everybody was pointing the finger at everyone else. My first thought was, *Oh hell no; something stinks!*

I had already had words with this same social worker who informed me (when Aunt Helen was first moved to the skilled-nursing unit) that Auntie was displaying signs of aggression. After being in a room alone for months, when Auntie woke up one day in unfamiliar surroundings and in a room with someone else, she was disoriented. She took her call button and whacked the resident in the next bed! The social worker called to inform me that if it happened again, they would kick her out. It wasn't what she said but the way she said it to me, which was real nasty, like she was enjoying having the power to say and possibly do something about it. Now I'm thinking that based on Auntie's past behavior they were sedating her to keep her quiet and calm and that's why she was lethargic and unresponsive.

After hearing about this latest incident, I wanted to make my presence known, and I couldn't wait to get there. I arrived in Detroit on an early flight. As soon as I got my rental car, I picked up Teryl and we went to the assisted-living home unannounced and got with this social worker and her supervisor. I told them I would report them to the Elder Abuse Hotline. Oh boy, that had them singing a different tune. Shortly after that, I began making arrangements to have Aunt Helen transferred to the same nursing home on the east side of Detroit where Aunt Margaret lived.

This trip I had an opportunity to spend time with Mom and to check out the house and see how things were going for myself. It appeared that she was staying close to the house and had stopped driving the car except to go to the corner store for a newspaper.

I noticed more and more that Mom's behavior was different: she wasn't remembering things as much, and she would get irritated with me if I corrected her. My heart fell to my knees; it was obvious that Mom had symptoms of Alzheimer's too! In November, I decided that I would take Mom home with me so we could spend time together and to give her a break from the cold weather. I thought it would be a nice vacation for her to be in a warm climate until the spring. She really didn't want to go, because she didn't want to leave her sisters. I had to lie and told her she would only be away for a few weeks. All was forgiven once she arrived in California and got to see her beloved son-in-law Darryl.

I was in such a hurry to get back home that I only took her essentials—a few items of lingerie, toiletries, and medications. I bought her new clothes when we got home. Darryl and I were working and had to come up with a schedule to try to minimize her time at home alone. Nothing in our house was familiar to Mom, and she would get confused leaving her room on her way downstairs to the kitchen. Darryl fixed her breakfast and lunch before he left for work and put sticky notes on everything for her from her meals to instructions on how to use the microwave.

She didn't know how to work the television remotes either. We had all the televisions on channel 7, so no matter what room she was in she could see her favorite program, *Oprah*.

Coming in from work one day, I noticed that Mom had been wearing the same outfit two days in a row. She was sitting in her favorite chair in the family room watching the television.

I asked her, "How are you, Momma?"

"Just fine, baby. How was your day?"

I responded that it was a good day and asked, "Honey, I notice you have on the same shirt and jeans you had on yesterday. Don't you like the new clothes we bought for you?"

"What new clothes? This is all I have." I took her upstairs to her room and showed her all of her new things. "Oh, I saw these clothes, but I thought they were yours." I was deflated. I didn't want to believe this was happening again.

I took her to my doctor for a checkup and asked him to review her medications. Mom had fourteen bottles of medicine! I originally blamed her doctor but later thought about it and decided that with Mom's condition worsening, she certainly did not realize that she was refilling the medication too often. After my doctor had the pharmacy evaluate the medicines, it was discovered that some of them were duplicates. We cleaned that up and continued her on a more streamlined medication regimen. I found out later that Mom's doctor prescribed quinine for her to help with the cramps she often got in her legs during the night, and I also discovered that quinine has a side effect of dementia!

One evening while watching television, I saw a commercial that showed a man confused and hunched over, walking slowly and shuffling his feet. The commercial indicated that he had neuropressure hydrocephalus (or NPH), which is a disease that mimics Alzheimer's. However, with NPH, fluid actually makes the brain swell, and once the fluid is drained into the stomach the person returns to normal. This procedure takes about forty-five minutes. I was actually hoping that this is what my mother had. I prayed that it was what she had so we could fix it and I would have her back to normal again.

My doctor ordered a CAT scan to determine if Mom was in the early stages of Alzheimer's. Darryl and I accompanied Mom to her follow-up appointment with the doctor, and after performing some additional tests in his office, he informed us that Mom was indeed in the early stages of Alzheimer's. This was the worst possible news for us. However, the doctor said that his diagnosis didn't mean that she wouldn't be able to function on her own. There were things we could do to slow it down; he prescribed a medication to help with that. I was determined to help my mother fight off the progression of this disease as long as possible.

Meanwhile, I finally had all the paperwork completed to transfer Aunt Helen from the skilled-nursing unit at the assisted-living home to the nursing home where Aunt Margaret lived. I didn't feel that I could trust them with her care any longer. After that, I relaxed a little bit, because I already had a good relationship with the staff at the nursing home and my experience with the way they treated Aunt Margaret was good.

Time seemed to be passing quickly. It was already the holiday season, and I was looking forward to my company's holiday shutdown. After I said good-bye to my coworkers and left to settle in at home for the Thanksgiving holiday, I arrived home from work and found that cars were parked in front of my garage and I couldn't get in to park my car. I was wondering what the hell was going on inside my house. When I opened the door, there was a party already in full swing! Darryl's cousin and her roommate came to town and stayed with us during the holiday. We celebrated Thanksgiving together, and the house was full of laughter, food, music, and dancing.

Mom was the center of attention, and she loved it. We partied, and it felt like the house had finally been christened. I was feeling some happiness for a change. After Thanksgiving, we shopped for decorations and put up the Christmas tree before our guests left to go home. When all the visitors were gone, the house was so quiet that Mom commented that she wanted them to come back because it was too dull and no fun. Hell, I don't know what she was talking about; I had to go back to work after Thanksgiving. I needed to get back in the work groove. Those women really knew how to party, and that's something I'm not used to doing anymore.

Darryl, Mom, and I had a very good Christmas, and I was happy she was here with us. Lily and Wallace were watching her house, watering plants, and picking up the mail, and Lily paid Mom's bills. We had a plan, and we worked it out. It really does take a village.

# Chapter Two—It's Time to Go

## 2005

We all welcomed in the New Year, I wondered what was in store and prayed to God that I would be ready to handle whatever came my way. I returned to work in January. I accrued a new bank of paid time off and tried to save every bit of it for trips to Detroit. Darryl and I overlapped our schedules so that there was only a thirty- to forty-minute window when Mom was alone in the house.

Since our house was alarmed, I couldn't feel comfortable putting the alarm on in the event Mom opened a door or window. On the other hand, I was afraid that she might open the door if someone rang the bell or just walk away. I called her constantly to see what she was doing and was always on pins and needles when she was alone in the house.

After a couple of months of getting up at 4:00 a.m., driving thirty-six miles one way and actually working, and then making the thirty-six-mile drive back home in "gridlocked" traffic (I believe Californians coined the phrase "gridlocked" because of the heavy traffic that plagues our freeway systems), this routine became a real drag. I was sleepy all the time, drained, and irritable. I seemed to be on the verge of tears all the time, and I can't leave out that menopause was rearing its ugly head too.

It was as though I was "on" all the time with no time to unwind. Here's where I thanked God I didn't have children in the mix too. I was always on the computer looking for answers and agencies that could provide any information to help me with the daunting task of keeping my mother safe.

During one of my searches through (believe it or not) my local phone book I found an adult day-care center about a mile from my house. I checked it out and thought it might be the answer to give me some relief from worrying about Mom being home alone. I took Mom to the day care, and while we were on the tour, Mom started acting funny; I could see her body tense up and the expression on her face change. The representative was explaining that they often went on shopping trips and to the movies and they did crafts, played games, and listened to music.

"Mom, don't you think it's nice here? Would you like to participate in the activities they have here?"

She looked at me like she could kill me and she responded loudly, "I'm not going no damn where with them, and I want to go home!"

I was so embarrassed. I know my face turned red, and I apologized to the lady showing us around and hustled Mom out of the building. And that was the end of that.

My husband was wonderful with Mom. You could see his love for her. He took care of her very well, and she adored him. I think she liked being with him more than with me. Really, think about it: she viewed me as the punisher, the enforcer. She even nicknamed me the "Gestapo." On the other hand he was the fun half, so she gravitated toward him.

When things start to change, I had to become the parent and ask her to do things that she didn't want to do. She would fight me all the way, because in her mind she felt that she could do for herself. I was still the child and she was still the parent! They don't want you taking over their bills, handling their money, cooking for them, and making them take the medicine they don't think they need. Taking them away from their home and belongings and asking them questions about anything agitates them and makes them resentful.

Mom seemed to be so lost. It broke my heart to see her just sit in the same chair watching television daily. Sometimes after I got home from work we would go for a walk and talk. During these talks, she explained, "Baby, I appreciate what you and Darryl are doing for me, but I miss my home and my sisters. I want to go home. I'll be all right." Besides that, she told me, "Cyn, you have a husband and your life to live. I don't want to be a burden."

As time passed I knew that these talks would get harder, because her comprehension and attention span would be all over the place.

Being with Mom daily seemed to put me in a weird space. Just knowing what her condition was and that it would continue to decline over time I think was depressing me. I felt like crying all the time, but I could only cry in the shower so no one would hear me. I felt like I had to stay strong, because if I didn't, who would take care of my golden girls?

As much as I loved my family, there were times when I felt resentful toward them. I began to ask, why me? I wanted to enjoy my life and not have to deal with all the problems that came along with taking care of these three ladies. The resentment in me became stronger every time another problem popped up. The best suggestion I have for overcoming those feelings is meditation, prayer, or perhaps even seeking help from a professional.

I prayed, meditated, exercised, and talked things over with my daughter and girlfriends to help me through these feelings. There were times when I wanted to give up and walk away. However, the rational side of my brain and my loyalty to family was strong, and that is what sustained me through this period of resentment and anger. These feelings had a tendency to dissipate once I saw my golden girls, and that would bring me to the reality that I was all they had to help them. In some ways, things got easier as I organized and sold off assets, consolidated, and prioritized things that had to be done. But with three of them to look after there was always something else to do.

In need of advice and at my wits' end, I called a longtime friend of the family and poured my heart out. I explained my dilemma with taking Mom back to Detroit or forcing her to stay in California, where I knew she was not happy. I begged him to help me. He said, "Cynthia, take her home. See how she does on her own, watch her carefully, pray all goes well, and then decide what to do." After we talked, I felt a sense of peace.

My intention was to keep Mom with us through the winter until April or May. But one evening while talking with Lily, Mom became very agitated and began to argue about Lily not handling her business correctly and saying that she didn't see why it was so difficult for her to just do what had to be done. She said, "I need to go home, because I never had to call her for anything when she went out of town and I handled her business. I need to go home and take care of my own stuff." When I intervened and tried to smooth things out, she lashed out at me. "Cyn, you don't know anything. I don't need you to tell me what to do. I'm grown!"

Things escalated and became heated between us, and then Darryl got into the fray, taking Mom's side of things (which, by the way, she loved), and it was them against me. "Honey, you shouldn't talk to Mother like that," he said.

I responded, "Look, Lily is a big help, and I don't see what Mom's beef is. I need her to calm down, because if she upsets Lily, and she decides to say the hell with this, I don't have anyone else to help me out! So you back up and let me handle this."

But no way was he letting it go. "I don't care. If you're too tired and need help, then I'll take care of it."

I told him, "If it was that easy you could have it, but right now, I'm going to bed."

Mom seemed to take pleasure in getting over on me, especially with backup. While Darryl and I were talking, Mom was sitting in her chair grinning and watching us argue like she was at a tennis match. She was very good at playing both ends against the middle. However, I was too stressed already, and the last thing I needed was to be embattled with my husband.

After the conversation with Lily and a phone call to speak with Aunt Helen, Mom said to me, "Listen, Cyn, I miss my sister, and I want to be home for her birthday in March." After that statement, she put her hands on her hips and said, "I'm ready to go home!" And that was that; I knew she would be a handful if I didn't take her.

We returned to Detroit in mid-March. Upon getting to Mom's house I noticed something amazing. My mother put her key in the door to her house, and when she opened the door, she simply said, "Dear Lord, this is my house and my things! You have a nice house, Cyn, but there is nothing like having your own. God bless the child who has his own." I would soon realize that taking her out of her environment and bringing her into mine where nothing was familiar to her and nothing belonged to her made a huge difference.

When Aunt Helen's birthday came around a couple of weeks later, Mom never mentioned it. That thought had totally evaporated from her mind. While Mom relished being back in her home around her belongings (which, by the way, she knew exactly how to work), she was taking inventory of her things, telling me that Lily had stolen her mop, stepladder, and silverware. Even after I showed her that those things were in the house, she remained angry with Lily.

Because of the materials I had read about Alzheimer's, I could see that her paranoia was ramping up. This put another wrinkle in the mix for me to deal with. Meanwhile, I had to go about my business and see how things were going with Aunt Helen and Aunt Margaret.

I will never forget receiving a call while I was driving down Livernois on a cold, rainy evening from a doctor at St. John's Riverview Hospital. He called to inform me that Aunt Helen had been admitted there, and after examining her and finding blood clots in her arteries near her heart, he recommended that she have surgery to implant a "green span" filter in her chest.

Before he finished his explanation, my head was spinning; I couldn't think straight. Making decisions for someone else's life is a heavy responsibility, and I was reeling. With what happened with Aunt Margaret and now Aunt Helen, these incidents gave me a whole new understanding of the saying "When it rains it pours." Hell, this was tsunami strength! There is no time for me to continue with those feelings. I have to make a decision quickly.

I told the doctor that I would have to do some research on this green span filter and get back to him. I called my doctor in California, and he explained it to me. I called Aunt Helen's doctor back that night and gave my approval for the surgery. I believe that everything happens for a reason. Bringing Mom home early brought us back to Detroit, so I could be with Aunt Helen through this surgery. And I was every day, talking to her, holding her hand, and comforting her. The surgery was successful, and Auntie returned to the nursing home a few days later. I was relieved and, needless to say, very grateful.

With Mom safely ensconced at home, a medication routine established, and once Wallace and Lily were looking out for and checking up on her, I returned home. I called Mom daily to check on her. One day during one of these calls she told me that she had been out for a walk. Trying not to sound alarmed, I told her that she should be careful when walking alone because of stray dogs (which ran rampant in the city) that run in packs. She told me that she was fine, and we went on to talk about something else. Wallace called me shortly after I finished speaking with Mom and told me that he went in the house to check on her and her coat was still cold; she really did go out that morning.

I thought nothing more about it. However, one day I got a call from a phone number in Detroit that I didn't recognize. I always answer anyway because it could be something important. In this case, it was. Selena, the granddaughter of my mother's good friend, called to tell me that her brother mentioned to her that he had seen Mom walking down the street in the bitter cold a few weeks ago with her coat unbuttoned and that he stopped to talk with her.

He asked, "Miss Alice, where are you going in this cold weather?" and she told him that she was on her way to church (which is a straight shot from her house to Woodward and a left turn to Pingree). He said that when she told him where the church was, it became apparent to him that she was lost; because she was on Byron and Woodrow Wilson by Hutchins Junior High School.

Thankfully, he and his uncle took Mom home and made sure she got in the house safely.

While Selena was talking, I was trying to come up with why Mom was on her way to church. We figured out that this incident took place the day Mom said she went for a walk, but it was in a different direction from where Mom told me she went.

A few weeks prior to her mini journey, she asked Wallace to take her to her church because they were having a celebration of choirs. (Our church hosted different choirs from around the city.) This event typically took place just before Easter, but Wallace had to work and told her he wouldn't be able to go. Mom knew the correct route to take, but we still don't know why she veered off the right path.

I was upset about this news and called my daughter. When Tonia and I went over the incident, I expressed my concerns that this "walk" could be the beginning of her walking away from the house and getting lost and not finding her way home. Tonia rationalized that she didn't think so, because Mom had a specific purpose in mind and knew exactly why she was leaving home.

Research is something I'm pretty good at, so I went into overdrive and found a program offered by the Alzheimer's Association called Safe Return. I ordered the materials, which included an ID bracelet with her name and health information, tags for her clothing, and most importantly a Safe Return ID number, which I could use in the event she went missing.

I had to provide the program with a recent photograph of Mom. Safe Return would distribute it to local law enforcement and the Alzheimer's Association upon receiving a call from me that Mom was missing, very much like the Amber Alert program. Once Mom had her ID bracelet and tags sewn in her clothes, I felt a little better. The good news was that after that first incident, she never walked off again.

Wallace would often take Lily and Mom to the store and run errands for them on his days off or after work. One day he called to tell me that his car had broken down and he couldn't get around to seeing them until he got it fixed; it was hard enough getting to work. When he told Mom about the car, she offered to let him drive her car again; no problem, she wasn't driving it anyway.

After Wallace took the car, things got back to normal with him taking them shopping and him coming over to see about Mom. Weeks went by, and one day Darryl and I got calls from his sister Barbara that Mom has been calling looking for Wallace. Mom told Barbara, "Wallace has stolen my damn car, and I haven't seen or heard from him. If you talk to him tell him to bring me my car!"

Here was another example of her paranoia getting out of control. Mom loved her little blue Toyota Corolla, it was the second car that she bought and paid for on her own. At this point, of course, she was no longer driving. She would ask Wallace to drive her car when he took her to the store, and she was okay with that, and even when Wallace's car wasn't running she would allow him to drive hers, before this latest incident.

But she had upped the ante on this particular drama. Alice knows how to put the "drama" in drama queen. Darryl called Wallace and told him to return the car and that would put a stop to all the calls to everyone in the family. Wallace was hurt that she told his family that he had stolen from her. Here's where I had to educate my brother-in-law on what he was dealing with and not who he was dealing with. He was hurt and very upset again when he and Lily and Mom were out and Mom vehemently cursed him and called him out of his name, apparently thinking that he was paying more attention to Lily than to her.

So I explained more about Alzheimer's to him: "Wallace, there are three stages that Mom will go through, mild, moderate, and severe. Right now, she's in the mild stage. She will progress through the other stages until eventually the disease takes over completely. She's taking medication that will help slow the progression, but it will not cure her." I told him, "Wallace, if you can, look deeper and find the person that you know her to be and not this new one that spews out foul words and accusations at us."

"Does she curse at you too?" he asked.

"Oh yes, and more." It seemed to comfort him some to know that she was treating me the same way. He nodded that he understood.

"I'll give you more information as I see her changing; just know that the changes will come eventually."

Wallace seemed kind of dazed, like he could not believe this was really happening to Mom too. After our talk, he continued to hang in there with Mom, even more protective than before. One thing I loved about Wallace was his loyalty to Mom; it continued to grow, and I believe in part that it was because he never forgot how she had his back when he was down on his luck.

Once Wallace returned her car, Mom resumed being the kind person she was, and they kissed and made up. She would call Wallace at work and tell him what to bring over for her to cook him dinner. When I called to check on her, she would tell me that she had cooked him Salisbury steak, mashed potatoes and gravy, and a green salad. Almost every day she said she cooked the same thing. Laughingly, I told Wallace that we would be rolling his fat butt down the street if she kept that up.

The months seemed to be flying by. Our vacation in May to Cancun, Mexico, was now a distant memory. It was back to reality and back to work. I was still paying bills in Detroit and coordinating whatever needed to be done there. Staying focused at work was getting much harder to do. I felt like Detroit's issues were consuming my conversation and every waking thought and that it was all I had to talk about anymore. My family and friends had the patience of Job, and I hope that I have told them over the years how much I appreciated them for standing by me.

One day in July I was checking Mom's bank accounts online. I noticed that $2,500 cash was withdrawn from her account! What the hell was going on now? I called her for an explanation, and she told me that she withdrew the $2,500 to pay for her bathroom renovation. I thought, *Okay, that's fine. She's still in the mode of fixing up her house, and that's a good thing. Right?*

Yes! Until she told me she was paying the neighborhood handyman $2,000 to do it. The hair stood up on the back of my neck! He happened to be in the house while I was talking to Mom, and I asked her to put him on the phone. I asked him to explain to me what he was doing for this money. The explanation did not satisfy me, and I got on a plane and showed up in Detroit with a great big attitude, ready to beat somebody down!

I looked at the shoddy job this guy had done that my mom had already paid him for, and I was very upset. I confronted this man and had him redo some of the work, but I was too late—he already had the money but not the skills to make it any better. Mom insisted that he had replaced her old tub. I explained to her that he did not replace the tub; he only put in a $300 tub surround. She believed him over me and actually got mad at me for questioning the man. The cabinet work he did was also subpar. Mom didn't want me to make trouble, so I let it go. I figured that once he left there, I would never see him again.

There's an important lesson here. Thankfully, having access to Mom's account allowed me to be proactive and check it frequently. I was able to catch this transaction before it could get any further out of hand. Watching her banking habits allowed me to take precautions and/or control when necessary of those accounts. (Mom had already added me and Tonia years ago.) If you do not have access to bank accounts, try gentle urging to get them to add your name. Try telling them that you can help them out by paying the bills for them and they can relax and enjoy retirement. If they are not able to handle their own affairs, consider going to court for the appointment to guardian and/or conservator.

If they are still able to conduct their own banking and paying the bills, suggest that they consider a power of attorney (POA). This will give you the authority, without having to go to court for an appointment to be guardian and/or conservator, to conduct their financial business later on when they become too incapacitated to do it themselves. The power of attorney expires at the time of their death. If they have a last will and testament, this will spell out their wishes on who is to conduct their business and how upon their death. When possible, consult an attorney.

In either case, be prepared to have them put up a fight with you about their money and losing control. My mother was an exception in some ways; because I am her only child, she always kept me informed about things she was doing (whether I wanted to hear it or not). After the incident with the handyman, I painstakingly went through Mom's files and piles of papers. I reviewed her credit card bills for any strange purchases. I opened and reviewed the mail that she received. I wanted to know what was going on and whether or not someone else might be trying to take advantage of her.

I constantly told her that if *anyone* asked her for money, she should give them my number and have them call me. I told her not to ever sign anything for anyone without speaking to me first. I frequently drilled this into her head. Telephone scammers frequently call senior citizens to prey on them with their schemes to cheat them out of their money. She assured me that she would, and I felt comfortable that she would, because if there's one thing I know about my mother it's that she didn't play when it came to her money. I was relieved. I returned home and went back to work.

My job was in turmoil, because by now the human resources (HR) department where I work was in training mode learning new compensation procedures for the upcoming performance-appraisal year. My stress level was through the roof, and I was run down.

I had so much on my mind that I wasn't sleeping at night; my mind didn't stop replaying events of the day, what I did and what I had to do. I always had the feeling that I was missing something, that I could make a mistake that could have been avoided if I knew more. My friends were telling me to stop beating myself up. I thought to myself, *Lord, help me stop this merry-go-round.* I felt like I was in the fun house, but this reality definitely was not fun. I felt myself being short-tempered and just not in a good space. My blood pressure was constantly high, and Tonia reminded me that hypertension is a silent killer, especially in African Americans. She suggested I take a leave of absence for a while. I didn't want to stop working. I loved what I did, and my coworkers made it fun to be at work. However, I told her I would consider it.

There is a saying that hindsight is 20/20. My advice to anyone who is a caregiver and still working is to be careful about how much information you share with your superiors (or coworkers, for that matter) at the job. Sharing too much information could backfire. Your employer may view the time off you take as a negative, even though it is time off you have earned. Let me explain what I mean.

I originally began working for a leader in the aerospace industry in 1983, in the human resources department. It was a good company that valued its employees and showed us by providing excellent benefits and retirement packages. I worked my way up to management positions and gained the trust and respect of higher-echelon executives in the company.

I was good at what I did. I worked in employee benefits, employee/ labor relations, personnel records, compensation, and ethics, as a liaison to the legal department, and in many other areas within HR. I was a supervisor, team lead, and acting HR manager on occasion. I counseled our top executives on policies, procedures, and personnel issues.

Once our company was sold and the new company took over, life as we knew it was a thing of the past. My manager began to hound me about going back to school to get a college degree. (I have a high school diploma, which pretty much means nothing these days.) He said he was "encouraging" me to get it because raises and promotions would be predicated upon degrees in the future more and more.

I don't know who he thought he was talking to, but I saw right through him. He already knew (because I told him) how much responsibility I had in Detroit, and my job duties at work were no joke. At some point I needed to have a life. It's called work/life balance. So there is no way in hell that I was about to take on something else to add to my stress.

Another reason he started to make this an issue was the company was looking for ways to cut costs, and long-term employees like myself cost the company a lot of money. Those excellent benefits I mentioned earlier were costly, and the company was looking for ways to cut those costs. The company was going in the direction of hiring younger personnel with degrees—at half my age, salary, and benefits. After a while, he got on my nerves, asking me what I was going to do about school. I continued to tell him it was not a priority on my list, and the battle was on.

I am an alpha female, good at my job and not by any means a pushover, and I am certainly not stupid (degree or no degree). He threatened my performance rating, which in turn would affect any future raises I might get, and that would impact my savings and retirement plans. If there was one thing he should not have done, it was to threaten me and my potential to earn money to take care of my family. I continued to work as usual, and we didn't have any more conversations about school for a while.

Commuting to Detroit had gotten really old by then, and I was always tired. For my next trip I decided I was going to take my time and not rush to squeeze everything that needed to be done into a week. So in September, hearing Tonia's words in my head, I applied for and was approved to take the Family and Medical Leave Act (FMLA). This leave is governed by federal law. The leave must be for a serious health condition of the employee or an employee's family member, and the guidelines define who qualifies as a family member. Employers must provide job protection throughout FMLA leave, and the employee must be reinstated to the same job he/she had before taking FMLA leave or a job of equal status, pay, and working conditions. An employee's health benefits are also continued during the FMLA leave. Personal leaves of absence do not have this federal protection. Check with your employer's HR department for additional information and to see what is required to apply for FMLA leave.

By October, I was back in Detroit to stay for six weeks with Mom, give Wallace a break, and handle other business that I could not delegate to anyone else. I had also seen a $5,000 withdrawal from Mom's checking account that I needed to look into.

I asked Mom about it, and she insisted that she had not withdrawn the money. I had already spoken to Wallace, and he couldn't tell me what she did either. He said, "I took your mom to the credit union and I went inside with her, but she told me, 'Wallace, I don't need you looking over my shoulder. Go wait in the car. I'll be right out.' So I left her there in the line and waited for her in the car."

A few days after I arrived, I took Mom to her credit union to investigate for myself. I had them pull the signature card and the transaction record. The young man in the credit union was going over the records with me, and Mom was interjecting her comments while I was attempting to explain the situation to him. I continued to query her about the withdrawal. By then she was irritated with me and jumped up and yelled, "This is my damn money, and I can do whatever the hell I want to do with it. You can't tell me what to do!"

Now everyone in the credit union was looking at us—specifically me! There I was dressed in fur and diamonds from head to toe, and they were looking at me like I was up to something shady. A hot flash went through my body, and I wanted to crawl under the table. Mom continued to rant, "You can't take my money; this is my damn money!" *Oh, my God, just shoot me now.* Now the guy helping me was looking at me as if he wanted to say, "Uh huh, stealing your momma's money." I was mortified. Mom finally settled down. It turned out that it was her signature on the transaction. She finally told me that she only meant to get $500, but she actually wrote $5,000. At that point, I knew I had to have a stopgap.

I put a password on her account (I figured she wouldn't remember it when they asked for it) and asked them to flag her account for any transaction over $200. They agreed to call me (after I explained Mom's illness), and that made me feel a little better that I had this under control. Check with your banking institution or credit union to see if they can accommodate special requests. What a day; after all that drama I needed a drink!

After the visit to the credit union we returned home and I went through Mom's house with a fine-tooth comb and found the money she had withdrawn stashed away in her hiding place. And much to my surprise, she had used very little of what she had withdrawn. I was very happy to have that mystery solved.

Mom's dining room was the hub of the house; it's where she watched television, ate her meals, paid bills, and talked on the phone all the time. Because she kept her personal information out on the table, anyone could see her personal business. I was concerned that someone could come in and pick up information about a credit card or bank statement.

Once again, I took my time and went through her paperwork and found overpayments on bills, lengthy automatic payments for things she had ordered from television infomercials, and some bills that were in arrears. Remembering that Mom had been handling her own business affairs for many years, I had to find the right way to approach her about taking over paying her bills to avoid these things happening in the future.

I had my work cut out for me, because she could be very stubborn. I explained to her what I had found and what needed to be done to make things better, I told her that I could save her some money (she perked up when she heard that) and avoid these overpayments and late fees from happening again. I simply asked her if she would *allow* me to help her with paying the bills. I think not demanding that she do it was the right way to approach this situation.

Having been independent for as long as she was, giving control to someone else couldn't have been easy for her. Much to my surprise, she didn't fight me and agreed without an argument. I cleaned it up and took it over and had her mail transferred to my house. If you have an elder who has been self-supportive, self-sufficient, and is still somewhat tuned in to what is going on, you must get creative in handling these matters of finance or any of their other business. They seem to dig in and fight you more when they feel threatened that you are trying to take control and leave them without their independence.

This was the first time I actually relaxed on a trip to Detroit, because this time, I was not feeling a lot of pressure. I was able to get things done without rushing; I was able to enjoy my family, friends, and Thanksgiving with my mom. Wallace and I rode downtown to look at the Christmas lights along Woodward Avenue, and they were beautiful.

I returned home in early December. After a tearful discussion with my husband, I went back to work and announced to my manager that I was retiring at the end of the year. His face hit the floor. He wasn't expecting that. Here's one chapter I was ending, not because I wanted to but because I had to. My health was becoming an issue, family matters were still intense, and something had to go. When I discussed it with my husband, his comment to me was, "Honey, you've given them twenty-two years. You need to take care of yourself and family now. It's time to go."

And so, after a retirement party that included past supervisors, friends, family, speeches, many recollections, and lots of pictures and tears, I closed that chapter of my life and walked away from a career that I loved very much. I settled in with my husband for the holiday season. Christmas was relaxing, and in many ways, I felt as though a huge burden had been lifted from my shoulders. Now I could turn my attention to seeking new adventures.

## 2006

I would normally return to work after the company's two-week holiday shutdown, right after New Year's Day. However, this January I was excited because the realization had begun to set in that I was free of my nine-to-five and my career as an HR professional was over.

I convinced myself that I had a chance for a new beginning, and I decided to finally pursue an education in interior design. I researched schools and enrolled in a design school in New York. I received my lessons via the mail, and this school allowed me to work at my own pace. This was perfect for me; in the event of an emergency in Detroit, I wouldn't be tied down to a classroom.

I was finally learning about something else that I loved to do. I wanted to prove to myself that I really was a diamond in the rough. Ever since my aunt Ruby allowed me to give her ideas on decorating her high-rise apartment in the Jeffersonian, I knew it was something I wanted to pursue, and now was as good a time as any.

One of my many job responsibilities at work had been to organize multicultural events. During our very first event, a Taiko ensemble (Japanese drummers) came in to play for us. They blew me away! This instrument was nothing like the cello I played in elementary and junior high school. I was very impressed with the young drummers, and I invited them back every year. After one of the concerts, I made an offhand comment to one of my coworkers that I would love to learn to play the Taiko drums. We laughed about it then, but the thought of trying it never went away.

Caregiving was so stressful at times that I wanted to do something fun, and even though I had no idea if I could really do these things, I decided to take the interior design course and play the Taiko drums. They provided a welcomed change from caregiving work, even though that really never goes away. I was going to Taiko class, and at the same time I loved my interior design classes and was doing well. There is a saying that if you do something that you love, you'll never work a day in your life. I felt that way about school.

Wallace called one day to tell me that he'd noticed a bad rash on Mom's hands and legs. He said that she had been sending him to the store for calamine lotion to put on it. I asked him what kind of rash it was; he said he doesn't know. But he suspected that she may have contracted it while she was planting flowers around the tree in front of her house and on her upstairs front porch.

A week later, I got another call from Wallace. He was franticly telling me that he needed to take Mom to urgent care right away, because the rash on her leg was now oozing pus and not looking good. I asked him to go ahead and take her to the doctor and get back to me. Later that day, Wallace called to say they treated the rash and gave Mom ointment for it and requested a follow-up visit. On this occasion Mom's poor judgment caused her not to make a rational decision, and she did not discern that the rash was worse and needed medical attention. Incidents had been minimal, and I was still not extremely concerned at this stage.

Months passed without major incidents, and if something minor happened, Wallace was there to handle the situation. He was still working, and things were going smoothly. Darryl and I took advantage of this lull in Mama drama; we took our RV out on a short excursion to Newport Beach, California, to enjoy time at the beautiful bay. These trips really made me feel like a retiree.

Traveling the open road, stopping where we wanted, when we wanted, meeting other RVers along the way—it was just a peaceful way to travel. In September, we headed out for Detroit to celebrate Mom's seventy-ninth birthday, and Darryl had a chance to visit with family and friends he had not seen in years. As usual, there were plenty of loose ends to tie up before we left. We stayed a few weeks and on our way back home visited family in the South. After we returned home, the remainder of the year was quiet, and we celebrated the holidays at home.

# Chapter Three—Never Done This Before

## 2007

As 2007 began I was excited to complete the professional interior design course. I enrolled in the next course, which taught advanced design, and had already received my first A. When I told Tonia about it, she congratulated me and then threw down the gauntlet, saying, "Okay, Mom, you've really set a high standard for yourself right out of the gate; now you have to keep it up." We laughed about the challenge, and I was excited to see if I could.

My happiness was short-lived. The nursing home called to tell me that Aunt Margaret had been transported to St. John's Riverview Hospital. I immediately contacted the hospital and was told that she was in emergency and someone would call me back.

The doctor's call dropped me to my knees, Aunt Margaret was *dead*! How could that be? No one had told me that she was sick. What happened to her?! I stopped hearing anything he said after that; it was like I was under water. A huge wave of guilt immediately engulfed me because I was not there; nobody was there, and she died alone. I cried like a baby. I felt like I had let her down. She passed February 27, 2007.

When I finally composed myself, I notified the James H. Cole Home for Funerals to pick up her body, made my reservations, and packed to go home and bury my youngest aunt. This would be a first; I had never buried anyone before in my life. That was something the older family members took care of. Here's a wake-up call for you—we are the older ones now.

Once the funeral home received her body, I got a phone call from Mom's longtime friend Mary, who, as it happens, had been working for the funeral home for many years doing hair and makeup for the deceased. Mary called because she recognized Aunt Margaret and she wanted me to know she would take care of her. She asked about Mom, and I told her that I was on my way home to tell her. I asked her not to call Mom until after I had spoken to her. It was imperative for me to get to Mom. I couldn't tell her this news over the phone—I didn't want her to find out that way.

After my plane landed, I went straight to Mom's house; she was in bed. I broke the news to her, and she took it better than I did. At first I thought to myself that maybe she didn't understand what I was saying. I asked her, and she replied that her baby sister was dead. She lay back down and went to sleep.

I thought that perhaps burying her parents and other siblings had given her somewhat of a shield against the pain of losing a loved one. When Mom finally woke up, it was as though I had never mentioned Aunt Margaret's passing. The next few days proved to be challenging for me, trying to keep my emotions in check so I could do what had to be done and manage Mom too. The experience of a funeral can be an overwhelming one. If you preplan for your loved ones and yourself, it is so much easier.

When I assumed responsibility for Aunt Margaret a few years earlier, I had contacted the cemetery and made arrangements for the opening/closing of the grave and the vault (a cement liner). I then sat down with the funeral director, Ms. Karla Cole at the James H. Cole Home for Funerals, and prepaid her funeral arrangements. Preplanning allows you to take care of the biggest things ahead of time.

At this point, I needed to concentrate on the funeral arrangements. I picked out a shroud for Aunt Margaret to wear and took them her underclothes. Yes, you must provide the funeral home with undergarments for them. They need stockings, panties, slip, and bra. Think of it this way (male or female): plan to dress them as though they were going out.

The next thing on my list was to contact the church where my family had been members for as long as I could remember. Mom and I visited with the church's secretary to get the program set up; this consists of what you want to say about your loved ones, a short synopsis of their lives, songs they may have loved, and speakers who will read the obituary, and don't forget to include a picture(s). The church was very helpful with suggestions and providing templates of past programs. After that, Mom and I went to the printer and the florist.

Since so many of our relatives had passed, Aunt Margaret's funeral was small. The long processionals we knew in the past were over. We were down to the last two, Aunt Helen and Mom. Aunt Margaret was a fun-loving woman. She loved dancing and music, drinking her beer, and having a good time. One of the things she loved saying the most was "Baby, it ain't the beauty; it's the booty." So I included that in her obituary. Mom was mortified about what the reverend would think. I told her I didn't care what he thought; this was about Auntie's life, not his, and people knew that to be something she always said. When the reverend read the obituary at the funeral service, he laughed at Auntie's saying, as did the rest of us.

Aunt Margaret was laid to rest March 5, 2007. I released six white doves at the gravesite. I didn't want her to be alone for this journey, and the six doves represented her mother, Addie Mae, her sisters Ruby and Fannie, and her brothers, William, Harry, and Freddy taking her home to be with them. Aunt Margaret, rest in peace.

The gravity of the death of her sister finally hit Mom, and she repeatedly spoke of missing her baby sister and how she had to bury her. It was sad, because at one point Mom made a statement that there was no one left. Her friends didn't call much anymore, there was no one to talk to, and she felt all alone and wanted to die too. I followed her closely to see if this depression would pass. A few days later, she was happy and moving about her business.

Because Wallace (or "Wally Gator" as I affectionately called him) was checking on Mom and helping her out, I was able to return to California and take care of their business from home. Just because I wasn't in Detroit that didn't mean that talking to attorneys, doctors, and caregivers stopped. I had two women who still need to be taken care of no matter where I was. Being home also gave me a chance to take care of my own business, which from time to time I had let fall through the cracks. I was so busy worrying about doing a good job taking care of their stuff that I was not doing what needed to be done for me and my household, and Darryl stepped in and took that over for me.

Wallace was invaluable in helping to take Mom to doctor's appointments and grocery shopping and taking her out for a drive. Whenever he felt he couldn't handle something, I would go home. But one day in June, Darryl told me he'd been notified that Wallace was in the hospital! I was scared beyond belief; Gator was my right-hand man. I immediately called him, and he said to me, "Don't worry, sis. I'm straight." What he didn't tell me was how severe his condition was or how long they planned to keep him in the hospital.

The next thing to cross my mind was that Mom was alone. How much food did she have? Who could I get to check up on her and make sure she had her medication? Hell, I needed to be there, so a few days later I was off to Detroit. In the interim, Mom was still managing to get dressed and prepare her meals. Lily was checking on her, and so was Carmen (Mom's tenant downstairs). There was enough food and other essentials in the house to sustain Mom until I got there. Meanwhile, I was in touch with her daily to track her whereabouts and her frame of mind. She did not have a clue that Wallace was sick, and I never told her that he was.

I learned over these years that anything that had a "bad news" connotation associated with it, Mom would blow out of proportion. Her brain's filter didn't keep things in perspective. For example, I happened to be in Detroit in October 2005, when Rosa Parks died. I witnessed Mom react to her death as though someone in our family had passed. She cried and was up all night long watching the funeral procession on television. She became so agitated that she began to fret that she had no money, about her bills not getting paid, that she had no food, and that someone was going to take her house away. She was at my bedroom door banging on it off and on all night long. No matter how many times I reassured her that everything was fine and she would be taken care of, she would retreat and return with something else.

Sometimes I used psychology on Mom to get her mind off a negative subject she was focusing on. I did that by redirecting her to something that was pleasant or funny or an event from her past that she related to, to distract her from what was upsetting her. In this instance, I finally got out of bed and joined her. We talked about the sixties and what a fun time we had in those days. With her mind on something else, I was finally able to change the channel, and she calmed down and went to bed. The next day I was worn out. But going along with them is sometimes the best thing to do to avoid agitating them further. There was no way I wanted to upset her by telling her that Wallace was in the hospital.

I got to Detroit in time to take Wallace to his first follow-up visit with his surgeon since he was released from the hospital. My concern was focused on Wallace being incapacitated. I surely did not want him to have any stress trying to care for Mom, and I needed to figure something out for her while he recuperated. One option was for me to stay longer; another was to take her to California. I was very reluctant to do that again, because I knew it would really upset her routine. Mom was doing well and was managing the routine that she had established for herself. But I noticed that her phone wasn't ringing off the hook like it used to. No one visited anymore, and since she stopped driving, she just sat in the house and tore up circular papers and old mail while looking out the front porch door.

She didn't want to venture out of the house to do things she used to do, like go to church, and even when I offered to go with her, she refused to go. I knew that Mom was aware that something was wrong with her, so she minimized contact with people to avoid embarrassment because she repeated herself constantly and was not always able to remember what was being said in a conversation. Anyone who knew my mom knew that she was very talkative and could be on the phone with her friends for hours. Before call waiting, I would have to dial the "O" for the operator to break in on the line to see if she was actually on it or if it was off the hook. Now seeing her sit in the house alone broke my heart, and I knew that she was missing her sisters and brothers the most.

When I mentioned to her about coming to California with me, she would say, "Cyn, you and Darryl have your life to live. I don't want to go to California. Detroit is my home, and this is where my sister Helen is. She needs me, and I can't leave her."

So I asked her, "What about me? I'm your daughter, and I want you to be with me because I love you."

She would just say, "That's right! I understand all that. I love you too, but Helen is my sister! We were born here, and I want to die here, in the city I love."

I got it. The strong sense of loyalty my grandfather instilled in Mom and her seven siblings was that you must take care of family. At first my feelings were hurt, but when I stopped to see it from her side, I could see that she felt that Aunt Helen needed her more than I did, especially since I had a husband. Mom still believed that she was in charge of her life and Helen's. So I shook off the feeling of being chopped liver and kept it moving.

With Wallace settled in at home and on the mend, I took Mom to Henry Ford Hospital for an evaluation to determine if she had progressed to another stage of Alzheimer's. When they tallied her test results, they had me in tears. The test was comprised of several scenarios: how she managed her money, if she knew how to contact 911 in an emergency, and other things. Apparently, Mom didn't pass the 911 test, and that caused the doctor some concern. He told me that Mom's Alzheimer's was still at stage one (mild), and he suggested that I think about putting Mom in a home.

"Doctor, I mean no disrespect to you, but this is the first time you have ever seen my mother, and you've only been with her for a couple of hours. I don't believe that warrants the diagnosis you're giving me. I see what and how she does things at home, and she's functioning pretty well. Perhaps you didn't ask your questions in a way that she could understand them."

He sat behind his desk with his hands folded in front of him in his pristine white coat and looked at me as though I was bothering him and responded flatly, "I understand how emotional this may be for you, but you should consider my recommendation."

To date, there is no cure for Alzheimer's. I was thinking, *Oh God, with so many of my family members affected, will this eventually be my fate too?* I began to freak out if I couldn't remember where I put my keys or if I said something and my husband would say, "You already told me that, honey." I was beginning to have flashbacks to when I said those very words to my mother and her flippant response would always be, "So I'm telling you again!"

I gathered up my mom, and with our arms interlinked we left the building. I was in tears, and as we walked back to our car, my mom patted my back, consoling me and telling me everything would be all right. I thought, *He can't be right. They don't know everything. Mom is just a number to him; he doesn't really care about her.* I determined on the drive home that I would prove him wrong. Since the doctor made a big deal of the 911 test, when we got home that day I tried a test of my own. While Mom was in the kitchen washing dishes, I casually asked her, "Momma, if I was hurt and you couldn't help me, what would you do?" She turned and looked at me like I was from Mars and said, "I'd call 911, silly." Lord, this was good news! I felt a sense of pride and relief.

I had to have my big-girl pants on when dealing with the medical profession, or attorneys for that matter. I was my own advocate. What does that mean? It means to look out for yourself and don't believe everything they tell you right off the bat. Ask questions, take notes, research what they say, and ask for second, third, and if necessary fourth opinions. Be sure to explore every option you have open to you before you take their word on such an important matter. I was not going to accept his word just because he had on a white coat.

Don't be afraid to push back! Just because they tell you to take a pill doesn't mean you should. Research it, asks the pharmacist about the side effects it could have on you, and ask if there are better or different alternatives. Ask about natural remedies. Please, educate yourself. Anyway, I mentioned the evaluation to Tonia, and she told me about a lady that my stepmother, Myrna, hired to conduct an evaluation on her mother to see how competent she was to live alone.

Myrna called and gave me the information I needed, and I contacted Diane Hiscke, RN.

Diane came out and spent several hours in Mom's home. During her interview with Mom, I sat silently in a chair observing and gave

Diane subtle nods when Mom did not answer correctly. Mom was very colorful with her explanations, and Diane went with it, letting the interview be totally about Mom. She asked Mom's permission for me to interject, and that kept Mom from getting angry at me; otherwise she would deny anything I said and become agitated.

Diane finished the interview and proceeded to check the house from the downstairs front porch to the upstairs front porch, each and every room in the house, asking questions along the way and asking Mom to show her how she did one thing or another. She completed her tour in the basement. Trust and believe she was thorough and all about her business. I was impressed.

Finally, done with the evaluation, Diane offered me her insights on how to make Mom's home safe for her to continue to live on her own. She suggested that I add hand railings to the downstairs front porch steps and to the stairwell down the back stairs leading to the basement. Remove throw rugs. If/when they start to shuffle their feet, this can be a trip hazard. Remove faucet handles and replace them with the push-down type that shuts off after thirty seconds to avoid running the sink over with water. The stopper in the sink should come out too. And install grab bars in the shower and a fire extinguisher in the kitchen. Diane praised the work I had already done on the house and went on to suggest that Mom needed to be more social, that she had too much time alone, and that solitude would only exacerbate her condition. Now I was thinking that this was a no-brainer. My spirits were lifted! Things weren't as dismal as the Henry Ford Hospital doctor painted them to be.

In 2002 Tonia and I had already scoured the city for the best adult day-care facility to take Aunt Helen to, and in my opinion that was the Senior Activity Center (SAC) Adult Day Care in Detroit. I was impressed by their facility and the way Ms. Parker and her staff took care of business. I called Ms. Parker and explained my situation. We met, and she gave me the appropriate forms that needed to be completed by Mom's doctors before she could start there. I told her that my mother would resist, and she told me not to worry, to bring her in once all the paperwork and medical test were complete. By the time I got through hauling Mom through the process of getting her TB test and completing her paperwork, I was exhausted!

Getting Mom out of the house so she could stay active was a key component in staving off the progression of Alzheimer's. She needed to stay engaged in activities, something as simple as washing dishes or folding the laundry. It was good for her to do things that gave her a sense of purpose. It may very well be frustrating to see her not doing it right the first time, and I may have to redo the chore, but the benefits would far outweigh any negatives. I only went over Mom's chores after she went to bed; otherwise she would fuss at me and tell me she didn't need my help.

Now that some of my concerns for Mom and Wallace had been allayed and some pressure lifted from Wallace, it was time for me to think about going home. But while I was running around visiting Aunt Helen, checking on Wallace and Mom, and doing anything else that needed to be done, I had an anxiety attack. I was looking forward to going home pretty soon, but just the thought of packing, returning the rental car, dragging my huge suitcases to and through the airport, going through airport security, and finally getting on a plane was overwhelming me.

When Darryl called to ask what date I wanted him to get my ticket, I broke down and cried. He cranked up the RV on July 19 to come and get me. This is just one of many reasons I love my husband dearly. Meanwhile, Wallace and I took Mom to see the center on July 23, 2007. The minute we drove up and opened the car door for her to get out, she went into fight mode. It was as though she suspected that we were up to something, and she pulled away from me and told me, "I ain't going no damn where!"

At that point I had to get firm, and I told her, "Mom, if you don't go in with us, we'll have to take you to the nursing home where Aunt Helen is instead of day care." Her demeanor changed immediately. I also explained that it would be fun for her to be around people her age. My mother has always been a very personable, social, fun-loving person, and she needed this; she just didn't know it.

I signed the paperwork and enrolled Mom that day. Ms. Parker did the intake interview and was very good at deflecting Mom's objections. When she got up to show Mom around and introduce her to some of the other clients, Wallace and I ran out like two thieves running from a robbery! We were giggling like kids! We had a leisurely lunch, and a couple of hours later we went back to get Mom. That chick never missed us! I guess the joke was really on us!

We had to establish a new routine for Mom, I stayed in my room in the mornings so Wallace could handle things. (He would be the one calling her during the week, and her routine needed to be established without me, because eventually I would return home). I also stayed out of the way in the mornings so I could observe what Mom would do and how she did it. Once she got her call from Wallace, Mom got out of bed, bathed, got dressed, prepared her breakfast, and waited faithfully by the front door for the center's van driver to pick her up. They picked Mom up in the morning and dropped her off in the late afternoon. It only took a couple of days for her to get in the groove, and she was off and running.

I was so pleased and relieved that the center was working out. Ms. Parker and her staff were very proficient and professional. They prepared continental breakfast in the morning and "hot" lunches every day in the kitchen right there on the premises. There would be no cold box lunch for my mother! They were even nice enough to send Mom home with meals for her dinner. Mom also got her medication during the day. I no longer worried about her being hungry or missing her meds. They cut her hair, did her nails, and took her on outings. Mom was enjoying herself immensely!

Mom attended the center Monday through Friday. On the weekends, she got up looking for the center's van driver to pick her up and would get mad because he wasn't coming. To appease her, Wallace would take her out with him when he did his errands and made his rounds to visit family. Now we couldn't keep her in the house; it was always "let's go go go!" Wallace and Mom's motto was, "C'mon, let's roll!"

Darryl had a grueling cross-country trip but finally made it to Detroit safely. I was glad to see my honey and the RV. It was our home away from home, and it felt good to be in it. Since Darryl had not been to Detroit for a while, we stayed on another week so he could see family and friends and we could make sure Mom was getting ensconced in her new routine of "going to the center."

We left Detroit on July 29 with my sister-in-law Barbara along for the ride. We dropped her off in Alabama to visit their dad. Then Darryl and I headed to Georgia to visit Tonia, Daddy, and Myrna for a few days. After our visit with them we returned to Alabama to spend time with his dad and his aunt. These trips were priceless, because everyone was getting older, and it was good to spend time with elders, listen to their stories, and help out where and when we could.

We stayed a few days in Alabama and headed back to California. We arrived home on our twentieth wedding anniversary day, tired but happy to be home. A couple of weeks later we celebrated my birthday. I was looking forward to some much needed R and R, and we took the RV to the Pechanga Casino and Hotel/RV Resort and went to see the Temptations and Four Tops in concert.

After being away from Detroit for more than thirty years, I had come to see a pattern when it came to phone calls and the time the call came in. I pretty much learned that during the day a call from the 313 area code was probably not going to be too bad. However, evening and late-night calls, not so much.

Late one evening in November, I was in the bed reading and Darryl was up watching television. I saw a call from Wallace come in on the caller ID. My husband talked with him, and a few minutes later Darryl asked me to pick up the phone. I suddenly got a knot in my stomach. I thought that whatever this call was about, it couldn't be good.

It was almost midnight in Detroit, and Wallace was at Mom's house. He was describing the scene there. "Sis, the police and crime scene investigators are at the house and have the backyard cordoned off. When I got here, your mom was on the upstairs back porch in the frigid cold trying to figure out why all these people were at her house." (She did know enough to call Wallace to come over.) Wallace continued. "Carmen was found dead in her car parked in the alley behind the house!" Whaat! I was stunned to hear about this.

Apparently she had gone to a friend's house to visit, and after they finished playing cards, Carmen told them she was going home and would talk to them later. A couple of days had gone by and her friends were unable to reach her on the phone. They came by the house to see if she was all right and discovered her car covered in snow, with her in it. She had a heart attack and died before she could get in the house. Carmen's friend gave me the phone number for her daughter. I called her daughter and expressed my condolences. We discussed moving out her belongings and how soon these things would take place. She assured me that everything would be out by the end of December.

My husband left home in November, right after Thanksgiving, and was in Detroit on business when he called one day to tell me that he could hear noises coming from downstairs that sounded like Carmen's dog, Jack. He said, "Honey, the last time I saw Carmen's daughter was the day she moved the big-screen television out. I haven't seen or heard her downstairs for days, and mail is piling up in the door." Darryl didn't have a key to the front door. I told him, "Kick the chain off the door from the basement and go in and check to see what's going on." He found Jack without food or water. The place was in disarray, with boxes everywhere. I contacted Carmen's friend and asked her if she would take Jack because I couldn't reach her daughter. She did. She also asked me what would become of Carmen's belongings. I told her if I could not reach Carmen's daughter to make arrangements in the next few days to get her belongings, I would dispose of them when I got to town. I prepared to leave for Detroit in January.

## 2008

We never did tell Mom that Carmen passed away, only that she was moving to be with her husband. When I opened the door and went into the downstairs flat, I was floored by the monumental amount of work that needed to be done to get it in shape to rent. After twenty-plus years of living there, Carmen had a lot of stuff. Her daughter had disappeared with Carmen's car, and we never heard from her again. By this time, Wallace had accepted my offer to move in downstairs so he could be closer to Mom.

I decorated the downstairs flat for Wallace, and he was happy with the way I had "hooked up" his place. I reminded Mom that Carmen had moved out, because she could no longer afford the rent and that Wallace had moved in so he could look after her. She was happy about it, or so it seemed. But—*oh snap!*—in February, Mom was looking for her rent money! Even with Alzheimer's, she was still tuned in to her routine of collecting her rent money every month. Mom kept calendars on the dining room table, and those calendars (some for past years) were her bibles. She had a lot of information on them to remind her when to pay a bill, celebrate birthdays, or watch a television show. And, yes, when the rent was due!

I tried my best to explain in the simplest terms I could think of how the arrangement of Wallace living there would go. But she didn't want to hear it and cussed me and Wallace out about her rent. She called Darryl and asked him to make Wallace pay her because he was taking advantage of her—another instance of paranoia was rearing its ugly head. Mom would tell me that someone had come in her house and stolen something, her telephone book, her mop, or her silverware, which she thought Lily took. But even though I knew that she was paranoid, I still had to think things through to weed out what could possibly have some truth to it. I never totally discounted all the things she told me, only the things I knew for sure were not true.

Finally I told her that I was collecting the rent and putting it in her account, and she complained about that too. Mom was used to keeping cash on hand for her pocket and buying groceries. She wasn't used to not having her rent money, and it was posing a problem. Eventually she let it go and would only bring it up on occasion. I thought about how it must be to feel helpless, without any money of your own, when for most of your life you had it and did what you wanted to with it. Now someone comes along and tells you that you can't have money, you can't drive, don't do this, and don't do that. I'm pretty sure I would feel the same way too. I decided to give her twenty, one dollar bills rolled up (it's what Wallace and I laughingly referred to as her "pimp roll") to put in her pocket. It made her feel better, and it made her feel that she still had some control. I always wanted her to have her dignity, and I never wanted her to feel humiliated.

I found that at times I had to use tactics to deflect an unhappy or angry mood, and that would change her focus to something positive. For example, I deliberately kept the television on programs that were comedic (and not the evening news) or involved dancing (something she loved to do) or were game shows (because she played along and knew the answers to the questions). She just loved the classic movie channels that ran familiar movies with movie stars whom she still knew and related to.

Part of my routine whenever I was in Detroit besides caring for Mom was my visits with Aunt Helen to make sure she was okay. (Wallace took Mom to visit her in my absence, and my friends, whom the staff didn't know, also visited her and reported to me what they saw.) During my visits I would feed her and talk with her, hoping that she might say something to let me know that she knew I was there with her. Needless to say, I checked her over to make sure she had no sores or bruises anywhere. Each time I visited, I was happy to see that Auntie was clean and well cared for by her attendants.

I had a good rapport with the nursing staff, and they always seemed happy but surprised to see me, only because they knew I lived in California. They used to tell me that they saw more of me than they did of people who lived right there in the city. Many of their residents had no one but the staff, and others had infrequent visits with their families.

If I happened to see something that was wrong, I brought it to their attention and followed up to make sure it was corrected. I found that when I did that, I was mindful of how I said things, because, as my mom always told me, "You catch more flies with honey than you do with vinegar." Contrary to that statement, there are times when you really have to be vinegar in order to get your point across. But either of these scenarios could put your loved one (whom you are leaving behind) in jeopardy. It is a tight rope to walk.

After refurbishing, decorating, and helping Wallace get settled into the downstairs flat I returned home in March. I was enjoying my classes, and I diligently practiced my Taiko drumming with the goal of playing in the upcoming June concert. At this point, I was thoroughly enjoying myself for a change. I played in the concert and was very proud of myself. I thought, *Here's a goal I can cross off my bucket list. What's next?*

Months passed without incident, and Mom and Wallace had a routine that was working nicely, and I was happy about that. Things were running like a well-oiled machine with them. Wallace never admitted needing a break, but I could tell it was about that time. I returned to Detroit in September to spend time with Mom. It was also getting close to her eighty-first birthday, and I wanted to have a small celebration with family and friends.

But before I get into that, I called Diane Hiscke, RN, again to come and reevaluate the house and Mom to see if she could remain on her own. The report came back that yes, she was still holding her own and that getting her in to social activities at the center was the best thing I could have done for her. I was very pleased. On that happy note, I turned my attention to planning Mom's party. My mom had said many times how much she missed her family. So I reached out to some of them and invited them to her party along with some of her friends and my husband's family. Mom was in her element, being the center of attention, and seemed to light up when her nieces and nephews showed up. Even though it rained very hard that day, the turnout was nice, and we all had a good time, just like the old days.

After the party, I noticed that the rash that Mom had contracted on her hands and legs was still a problem. Her legs had healed, largely because she could not see the rash to scratch it. However, the rash on her hands was in prominent view, and she continued to pick at them. It had worsened beyond belief, and my mother's beautiful brown skin looked as though she has been char-burned.

Wallace and I had taken her to numerous appointments with a dermatologist. They told us that the skin would continue to thicken as long as she picked at it. We tried creams, lotions, ointments, bandages, cotton gloves, and everything else we could think of to deter her picking, but to no avail. And what was even worse was that she had started to pick her face. Mom said her hands didn't hurt or itch; she was just trying to pick off the scab to get her skin tone back. No matter how the doctor and I tried, we could not convince her to stop. It is sometimes very hard to reason with someone who has Alzheimer's, so I had to be innovative and try to outsmart her. But on this one, I had to admit I was out of tricks! To regroup and refresh my brain, after one of her doctor appointments I had to take a break. I didn't want Mom to feel I was continuously beating her up about the rash—she needed a break from me too. So to perk us up, I decided to take her for a ride.

I loved to see my mom smile and hear her talk about her past. To help her invoke those memories, I took her to Belle Isle (an island that sits in the middle of the Detroit River), and we rode around the park admiring the landmarks and reminiscing about old times. We stopped at the ice cream truck, and I bought ice cream cones that we ate while we sat and watched ships glide through the water, Mom would tell me how much she wanted to get all the family together and have a picnic like we used to back in the day. I didn't have the heart to tell her that family as she knew it was just a memory. She had planned it all out in her head: who could bring what dish and how much money we would save if we went to the Eastern market and bought in bulk quantities. Amazing, she seemed to be her old self again. These moments were precious, and I learned to hold on to and cherish each one.

I returned home six weeks later and continued to excel in my interior design classes. At this point, I was a straight-A student with many awards to my credit for my innovative designs. My dean of studies said that he had never had a student with my insight into design and that I should do well on my own, and believe me, I was anxious to try. My classes were about to conclude, and I submitted my final exam and thought, *Now what am I going to do?*

Darryl and I celebrated quietly at home for the holidays without fanfare. Another year was approaching, and we were both praying for peace.

# Chapter Four—Patience Was a Virtue

## 2009

### Florence "May"ola

Our family was spread out and getting smaller. I tried to keep in touch with my elders and visited them when I was in Detroit. My eldest cousin Florence (we call her May, short for Mayola), seventy-eight years old, and her husband were the only other family members still living in Detroit whom I kept up with. May was my mother's eldest sister Ruby's daughter. She was an only child, and she married her longtime sweetheart; they had no children.

May was slender, very stylish, and always looked good in her clothes. She was intelligent and worked as a registered nurse for many years. But she wasn't always the most pleasant person to be around, and we had a tendency to avoid her. I recall that under that prickly exterior, from time to time she allowed her softer side to show. It was as though she always had a chip on her shoulder—as though she had something to prove—and I never figured out why.

Nevertheless, she and her husband were still family. May held a grudge against my mother, Margaret, and Helen, because when Aunt Ruby passed in 1998 she left each of her remaining sisters some money. May told me that the sisters coerced her mother into giving them the money that she said was rightfully hers. This incident caused her to stop speaking to the sisters for a long time. Even with this history, I continued to visit her or at least call whenever I was in town to take care of the golden girls.

Let me fast-forward to March 2009. I called May at least once or twice a month. On one particular occasion, I called and a woman I did not recognize answered the phone. I was surprised, because May rarely had visitors. I asked the woman if I could speak to May. When May answered the phone, she didn't sound like herself.

I asked her, "Hi, cuz, how are you?"

"Cynt, is that you?"

"Yes," I said. "Who is the woman who answered the phone?"

May responded, "That's Sharon."

"Why is she there? Is everything all right? Where's your honey?"

She responded, "He's dead!"

I said, "May, stop playing. It's mean to say things like that," and she said it again. I asked her again who was the woman who answered the phone, and she said her longtime next-door neighbor. I asked May to put the woman on the phone again, and I introduced myself.

She said, "Hi, Cynthia. I'm Sharon, and I live across the street. I know who you are; you're Alice's daughter." I still didn't remember her.

Sharon continued. "Yes, May is correct—he's dead."

I asked when this happened and why no one called to inform me. She said that he had passed the week before and that the funeral was the next day. She told me, "I saw that your number was on the refrigerator, but I thought someone else had called to tell your mother and that she would tell you." Oh, boy! Now I was beginning to understand why Mom was saying things about May's husband that I thought were weird.

Mom had difficulty articulating exactly what she had been told, and in hindsight, I think that her ramblings were what prompted me to call May that day. I listened very carefully to what my mom said, and I never disregarded her comments. I may have to piece them together to see if I can make sense of them, but I always listen to her.

The question on my mind was what was going to happen to May. I asked Sharon, "Who is taking care of May right now?" She told me a friend of May's, Nikki, was in charge. Without her husband, May was all alone in this world. This friend was not her blood relative (her mother and May worked together, and Nikki grew up around May). I was not sure of her intentions regarding May's care. May was disabled because of a stroke she had some years ago and required assistance. I asked Sharon to have Nikki call me.

Meanwhile, I contacted my friend Winnye and asked her to check on May, meet with Nikki, and give me her best first impressions of her. She met with Nikki that evening. After she met with Winnye I had a telephone conversation with Nikki and asked about her plans for

May, and she stated that she would look out for her. She had made the funeral arrangements and was still formulating a plan to help May. I told her I would have Winnye hire someone to come and stay with May until something definite could be worked out.

She recounted that May had called and told her that she could not wake her husband. Nikki said that she told May to call the next-door neighbor Travis to help her because she was out of town. When the neighbor got to the house, he found May's husband unconscious. The EMS was called, and he was transported to the hospital where he died the next day.

After our conversation, I had a slight sense of relief. This woman sounded like she had a good head on her shoulders. She was fifty-one years old and had a job (in car sales), a house, and a car, and I recalled that May had always spoken highly of her. Winnye's assessment from seeing her in person was that she did not appear to be on drugs or alcohol and she seemed to be a clean-cut working person. The funeral was the day after our conversation. Of course, because I didn't know about the funeral ahead of time, I was unable to attend. I booked a flight and got there the following week.

While I was waiting to leave, I called May daily and spoke to a male nurse Winnye hired named Benny. May seemed to like him, and Nikki was holding things together and meeting May's needs. When I arrived in Detroit, Wallace and I went over to see May. I rang the bell and was met at the door by Benny. He told me he had instructions from Nikki not to let anyone in, and even though I told him that he and I had spoken on the phone and that I was May's cousin, he still refused to let us in. My heart started pumping faster. He then shut the door in my face; I was about to blow my stack!

What the hell was really going on in there? Were they doing something to May? Where was she? I called Nikki's cell number and got voice mail. I left a message saying that if she didn't call this man and have him open the door immediately, I would call the police.

I rang the bell and knocked on the door again. Benny answered, and I could hear May calling, "Is that you, Cynt?"

I said, "Yes it's me, cuz. Are you all right?"

May told him to open the door, and I heard him tell May, "I have my instructions. If you want to let her in, then you have to get up and open the door, because Nikki said no one is allowed in here without her permission."

May yelled at him, "This is my damn house and she doesn't tell me what to do in my house." She came to the door, and when we got in, words were exchanged between Benny and Wallace and things got really heated really fast. I stepped in and asked them both to calm down; there apparently had been a misunderstanding.

A short time later, Nikki called and apologized, stating that Benny had overstepped his boundaries and that his instructions did not include May's family, just curious neighbors whom she didn't trust. Nikki shared with me that she had discussed with May her going to court to become her guardian and conservator. She said it was difficult for May to really grasp what needed to be done; because of her memory loss and delusions she still believed that she should be in control and could take care of herself. I thought, *Wait. Did I hear her right?* "What do you mean May has memory loss and delusions? I speak to her often enough to tell if she's not herself, and she always sounded like she was in her right mind to me."

What she told me next broke my heart. "Her husband was in denial about her condition, but May was diagnosed a year ago and is in the early stages of Alzheimer's." She said that she appeased May by telling her that once she had time to go through her grieving period and felt better that she could take things over again. May reluctantly agreed. Nikki was scheduled for a court appearance soon, and I told her I planned to attend on behalf of my mother and myself since we were May's next of kin.

We appeared in court, and I told the judge who I was and that I did not have any objections to her appointment at this time. The judge appointed her guardian and conservator. However, a few days after that, she called to tell me that she couldn't do it!

She had already told the court that she didn't want to be burdened with this kind of responsibility. She said, "I'm sorry, Cynthia. I don't mind helping out, but I'm planning to get married next year, and I'll have three stepchildren to take care of." When she finally took a breath, I told her she'd have to do what she felt was right for her. Now I was in a quandary, wondering once again what was going to happen to May.

I talked it over with Winnye, and she advised me to let it go and let the courts find someone to take care of her. "Cynthia, you've done so much already. You have to think about yourself and Darryl. Think about how taking her on will affect him too."

I told her, "He understands family. He'll be all right if I decide to help her."

On my way to the airport on March 24 I received a phone call from an attorney for the court. She told me that she had spoken with Nikki and that she declined to accept the appointment to be May's guardian and conservator. She said that the judge asked if I would be interested in taking over those duties. I told her I would, if the judge would stipulate that I did not have to return to court for another hearing or to file the paperwork since I was literally on my way to the airport to catch my plane to go home. A few days after I got home, I contacted Nikki and told her that I had accepted the successor guardian and conservator roles, but it would be a few weeks before I received my official documents.

Meanwhile, I told her that I needed to know what was what and where things were with the day-to-day household operations, the bills, May's care arrangements, etc. I also told her to make sure she kept all receipts for any money that she spent in the interim, and I asked for an accounting of the bank accounts and credit cards. She gave me some bank balances over the phone and promised to mail the other information I requested.

My attorney sent me the official guardian and conservator court papers in May. At this point, I was able to take over the bank accounts and add my name to these accounts so I could officially pay bills. Two weeks after I received my documents, I located a Comerica bank approximately twenty-five miles from my house. May also had an account with Chase bank; however, I could not conduct business in a California Chase bank, because they were not connected to the Chase banks in Michigan at that time. I would have to return to Detroit to handle business with them. I was already hearing Winnye's voice in my head telling me, "I told you not to take on any more work."

On June 2 I went to the Comerica bank, sat down with the vice president, and gave her all my court documents, and she in turn faxed those documents to the branch manager at the Comerica bank branch in Detroit handling May's account. Now that I was official, I went home and reviewed everything that Nikki had mailed me. I called the Comerica bank to get a current balance on the account and was stunned when the operator told me that there was very little money in the account. I can't believe it! What the hell happened to the other money that was there? Red lights, bells, and whistles went off in my head.

I was informed that a check was made out for a large sum of money in the name of and cashed by—you guessed it—Nikki! I could only breathe fire at this very moment. I went into overdrive and told the operator that I needed a fraud alert on the account immediately. Ironically, Nikki had cashed the check the day before I went to the bank; that's how it got through. Otherwise, the conservator designation would have put up a red alert to the bank and they would not have cashed it.

At this point my mind was spinning! I contacted the Comerica branch in Detroit, where the branch manager and I had a rapport. I explained the circumstances to her and had her pull all the checks paid and make copies for me. I also contacted May's Chase bank branch and spoke to the branch manager there. This woman was so incredibly nasty that I wanted to go through the phone and throttle her.

I fervently explained to her that I was only trying to prevent any misappropriation of funds, and when I finally got through to her, she agreed to put a flag on the account until I got there. I got it—she had no idea who I was or if I was trying to pull a scam; identity theft is rampant these days, and thieves have all kinds of tricks up their sleeves. That same day, I had a reservation for a flight to Detroit. I arrived in Detroit June 12 and went straight to the Comerica bank to pick up the check copies. I also went to the Chase bank to lock that account down. As a precaution, I had the old account shut down and opened a new one.

I spoke with Nikki to let her know that I was in town to celebrate May's birthday but that we needed to meet so she could give me everything she had that belonged to May. The next day, Nikki and I had dinner and pleasant conversation. I asked several times if she had all the documents I needed—receipts for money she had reimbursed herself for, car registration, medical cards, insurance information, checkbooks, etc.—and she handed me a file folder of items. I went through the file and asked about missing items she should have had. She explained that her boyfriend had recently moved in with her and things were still a mess but that she would get them to me.

Just as the server was clearing our table, I produced my file folder with the check copies I had gotten from the Comerica branch manager, specifically the one indicating the large withdrawal. I showed it to her, and her face hit the floor! I asked her what she spent the money on, and she answered me in a raspy whisper. I had her repeat what she'd said: "I, uh, paid for the funeral expenses."

I replied, "Okay, that's fine. I'll need the receipt for that, and I need it by tomorrow, because the first fiduciary accounting is due next month." She said she would drop it off at May's house the next day. After more than a week with no response, I lost my temper, and the phone message I left her was full of expletives. She called twenty minutes after I left the last message, telling me that she had been working late and had not found what I needed, so I gave her a few more days.

Meanwhile, I wasn't sitting on my butt waiting for Nikki; there is more than one way to skin a cat. I called Ms. Karla Cole at James

H. Cole Home for Funerals, and she was gracious enough to meet with me the same day I called her. I explained the situation, and she pulled her file on the service. I wasn't the least bit surprised when she told me that she had not received any money from Nikki. Funeral expenses were prepaid in 1994, and to add insult to injury, there was still an outstanding balance for the minister's fee and programs. Before I left, I paid the bill and thanked Ms. Cole for her time.

The next day I drove out to the cemetery and met with the manager there. He produced his records and showed me that everything for both May and her husband had been paid for since 1974 and there was no balance owed. My next stop was the Detroit Police Department to file a complaint of fraud against an incapacitated individual.

As a court-appointed conservator I was responsible for May's finances, and the court required me to submit an accounting of how her money was spent annually. Because I was a successor (meaning I took over the title and duties her husband had after he passed), I was at a disadvantage. To compound matters, Nikki had control of May's finances for at least three months before I took over, and she had not kept good records of her spending. The court also required me to be bonded to handle her assets. This means that my personal funds would be used to cover May's assets. If the court found that I have misappropriated her money, they would take that money from my savings and retirement monies. And I was definitely not trying to hear that!

It was incumbent upon me as a caregiver, guardian, or conservator to do my best to investigate wrongdoings. So the fight was on. I was determined to get to the bottom of where this money went and why. I was not going to take any blame for Nikki's alleged thefts. And I would make sure she knew that I was not the one to play with when it came to me, my money, and my family! I was full of rage, knowing that someone was stealing from a helpless person in my family. This was stuff I read and heard about on the news, never thinking that it might happen to me or someone I know. So let this be a warning to all of you in my position to take precautions to protect yourself and your loved ones the best way you can.

These days thieves are really slick. We know that they have many ways to cheat, lie, and steal from you, but one thing is guaranteed: if you don't do something to protect yourself by doing just one little thing to slow them down, you'll make it easy for them. For example, once I had control of the bank accounts, I closed the old ones and opened a new account. That way, I could be assured that any missing checks from the old account could not be cashed.

Additionally, I ordered credit reports from Equifax, Experian, and TransUnion to check credit balances and credit card activity. I used a cross-cut shredder and destroyed any documents with account numbers or other personal information. Thieves scour trash cans set out on the curb for this kind of information. The worst thing is that you also have to keep an eye out for those who are close to you, because it's not always a stranger; so-called friends and family can be treacherous too.

I interviewed the caregiver, Benny. He was still caring for May and was, as far as I could see, doing a very good job. May seemed to still like him, and we had moved past the chaos of our initial meeting. We were now communicating very well. I explained that he was not to take any instructions from Nikki; they would all come from me along with his paycheck. I asked if he wanted to stay on with us, and he explained that he was all about taking care of May and was studying to become a registered nurse. He said that he and May talked about her career in nursing and he had learned a lot from her; they bonded well. He assured me that I didn't have to worry about him.

Of course I was skeptical, but Winnye had checked his references thoroughly and found that he came highly recommended. He proved himself many times over, and he was forthcoming with information when I questioned him to see how much he knew about what Nikki was up to. He remained May's caregiver, and I gave him leeway to do his job in my absence. We were in touch daily, and Wallace was there as my backup, popping in unexpectedly to check on May and the house and to run errands for them.

I was happy that Benny stayed on, because in May's neighborhood, it was important to have a male presence around the house. When May moved into her two-story brick house in the early sixties, the neighborhood was well kept. Neighbors sat on their porches and waved as you walked by, but with the population aging that's no longer the case. Seniors fear for their safety and seek the protection of their homes. Now the neighborhood was marred with urban blight, vacant lots, boarded-up houses, and dope houses that stuck out like ugly sores on both sides of the block. My first instruction to him was to keep Nikki out of the house because she was no longer welcome for any reason. And she was not allowed to speak to May. If she showed up, call the police. Period.

After gathering as much evidence as I physically could while I was there, I left Detroit in the latter part of June and headed home. When I got home and settled down, I turned my attention to working on my business to get it up and running. I also wanted to continue educating myself on the staging piece of my business. To that end,

I joined an organization of home stagers and attended my first meeting in July.

Just as I was about to walk into the meeting, I received a call from Ms. Parker. She called to inform me that Mom's appearance has been disheveled lately and she had a body odor. She questioned whether she had been bathing. I told her that I would talk to Wallace and get back to her.

Moms' two-family flat home is pretty old, and the walls are thin and the floors creak; while this could be annoying, it turned out to be a blessing that allowed Wallace to hear what was going on upstairs. Wallace told me that he had been calling Mom in the morning as usual and he could hear her get out of bed and walk into the bathroom. But he admitted that once he heard her do that he went about getting ready for work and did not remember if he heard the shower go on.

I asked him to pay closer attention and see if in fact she was using the shower. He called me back the next day and said he did not hear the shower go on. He went upstairs to investigate and found that Mom's shower was not working. He found her putting her clothes on over her pajamas. She refused to change into her street clothes and fought him when he tried to keep her from getting on the van to go to the center.

We had no idea how long the shower had been inoperable, but I immediately had someone go to the house and repair it. Once it was repaired, Wallace found that the routine had been broken and he was now unable to get Mom to take a shower. She would tell him she already had one. He called me distressed and asked me to come home and help him.

My stress level was off the charts. I had a lot to do. But no matter, because when Wallace said he needed help (which he rarely did), I responded to him as quickly as I could. I informed Ms. Parker about what happened, and she told me not to worry; she would assist Mom once she got to the center with her hygiene and dressing. This was the Band-Aid fix I needed until I could get there. Wallace took extra clothing to the center so Ms. Parker could change Mom. I knew Wallace was uncomfortable when it came down to this hygiene issue, and rightly so. Mom was not going to let him near her in that regard.

Ms. Parker and Wallace figured out a way to get Mom back into the routine of showering. After the shower was repaired, Ms. Parker told Wallace to remind Mom of what she was supposed to do in the morning. He went upstairs to wake her and turned the shower on. When she got out of bed, she got right in the shower, and after a few days like that, the routine was reestablished. Thank God, it was one less thing for me to do. Once again, I thanked God for blessing Mom and me with Ms. Parker.

My first fiduciary accounting (May 7, 2009, through May 6, 2010) was due to the court in July 2010. I had to get started on it early, because it was going to be a nightmare. Receipts and other supporting documentation were missing, and the theft would also present a challenge. My attorney was aware of the theft and assured me that the judge would not penalize me for something I had no control over. We'll see.

The way the accounting worked is that the attorney reviewed my submittal and eventually submitted the accounting to the court. The court appointed an attorney who was referred to as a guardian ad litem (GAL). This attorney was selected from a pool of attorneys to represent the court and the incapacitated individual. The attorney reviewed the annual accounting to see if there were mistakes and more importantly any malicious embezzlement. Once the review was completed and their report was submitted to the court, a petition had to be filed with the court to request a hearing, and both attorneys had to appear before the judge for his ruling.

The judge would either allow the accounting the way it was submitted or decide to amend it, keep the current conservator, or remove the conservator (due to malfeasance) and appoint a court conservator to take over on behalf of the incapacitated individual. I am by no means proficient in matters of accounting. Oh, I do well enough to conduct my own business, but being a conservator is a whole different animal. I was fearful that I would miss something and the court would think I was trying to be slick.

While I was trying to navigate my way through the accounting, I was also constantly on the phone with the police investigator, giving her information and trying to stay updated on her progress with my fraud complaint and her investigation. At one point, I was not reaching her at all. Weeks passed and finally I got her on the phone and she told me that she had transferred my case to another precinct. Whaat! I guess it was too much for her to call and tell me that, since I had been waiting for weeks.

So I contacted the new investigator and explained the case to her. She seemed annoyed, like I was bothering her. I was frustrated with this attitude, but I needed her. She requested items of evidence, and I faxed them to her. More weeks went by and I heard nothing from her. Each time I called her, I had to explain who I was and why I was calling. My frustration was building; time was moving fast, and I was not sure if there was a statute of limitations on fraud.

Even when I was not in Detroit I continued to work for Mom, Aunt Helen, and May. Mom and Aunt Helen's business after years of organizing was pretty much under control. May's business, on the other hand, was a Pandora's Box. I paid her bills and prepared the payroll for her three caregivers each week. It became a job.

I sorted through insurance papers and filed claims to get monies that were due her. I also went to the Social Security Administration (SSA) to file paperwork to become her representative payee to give me the authority to handle her social security benefits (cash/deposit the check, spend the money). The application delved into my background, and their approval was required before I could become the representative payee. An annual report is also a requirement, indicating how I spent the money received throughout the year. Although I had been appointed by the court in the state of Michigan as her conservator, the federal government trumped state government, and that appointment had no weight with the SSA.

While I was in the SSA office completing this paperwork, the man at the window assisting me told me that May's last name was different from what I gave him. In disbelief, I looked at what I had written and assured him that there was no mistake. He insisted that the name on their records was correct. I couldn't believe this. Where the hell did this other name come from? I left the social security office that day frustrated and bewildered because I had another issue to resolve, which, as it turned out, was just one of many.

I called May on the off chance that she just might be able to tell me something about this name change that occurred in June 1960. I had been through all of her paperwork, and there was nothing that indicated that she was divorced from her husband and married to someone else. And this name certainly was not her maiden name or her father's last name. May said she didn't know anything about a name change. I asked May's friend, who had been around her since they were in nursing school, and she said she never knew May to change her name. I also contacted my father, and he knew nothing of a name change or a second marriage. I returned to the social security office and concluded my business with both names on her record until I could sort it all out. Now I was thinking, *What's next?*

I was preparing to return to Detroit when I got a call from the police investigator, who told me that she was going to set up an appointment for me to meet someone in the prosecuting attorney's office and that he would be the one to decide if I had a case that had any merit. I told her that this was good news, that I was planning to be there on December 23. She told me to contact her as soon as I get off the plane and perhaps we could meet before she went home that day.

When I arrived in Detroit, my friend Debbie was waiting outside for me at the curb. As soon as I got into the car, I called the investigator. When she answered the phone, she sounded distracted and told me she would call me back. She didn't. To make matters worse, when I got to the house, Wallace told me that he did not receive the paychecks for the caregivers. I had mailed them in plenty of time for them to arrive before their payday, but they were lost somewhere. So I reissued their checks. I already hated that trip; it was not getting off on the right foot.

I called the investigator the following day, only to be told that she was out of the office for two weeks! I asked the officer if she had left any information for me regarding an appointment with the prosecuting attorney's office. He told me no, she didn't. What the hell? What was really going on? I was more than frustrated. What kind of game was she playing? I was planning on being on my way back home in two weeks, but I didn't come this far to meet defeat. I called my husband to tell him that I was going to wait this out. I needed to and would see this through. I had all my ducks in a row, and I wanted someone who could do something about it to hear my story.

This trip began with disappointments; but I decided that I was going to try and make the best of things. I pushed my disappointment aside so I could enjoy spending time with my mom, Aunt Helen, May, and Wallace, and the rest of my family and friends. But the holiday was bittersweet for me because I already missed my husband very much.

For the first time in many, many years, I put up a Christmas tree and lights in the window and I prepared dinner for Mom, Wallace, and me on Christmas Eve. The living room windows were steamed up, and the house had a cozy look from the twinkling colored lights inside the house. Outside, the ground was covered with sparkling snow. We lit candles and put them in the fireplace, hung stockings on the mantle, put our presents under the tree, and filled the house with Christmas music. Wallace came upstairs Christmas morning, and we had a good time opening presents.

On New Year's Eve day, I started preparing my dinner for the next day. In Detroit, the gunfire started about 9:00 p.m. on New Year's Eve. I guess the train of thought is that it must be 12:00 a.m. somewhere, and believe me, the residents in this city are well armed. I turned out all of the lights and moved away from the windows in the house and stayed low. It was very scary to hear rounds of ammunition going off continuously and well after the New Year had officially arrived.

I imagined that war sounded this way. I'm not talking about pop, pop, pop; I'm talking about boom, boom, boom! Mom and I huddled in her room, because her bedroom did not face the street or back alley and was the safest room in the house. Wow! What an entrance into the New Year. If these fireworks were an indication of what the New Year would bring, I was in for a ride.

## 2010

Finally, the police investigator was back from her leave, and I had a meeting scheduled with her. When I left the house on the morning of the meeting, the weather was sunny, windy, and downright cold. The street was pretty deserted, and I was anxious to start my errands and get back to the house. When I started the car, it made a horrific noise. I thought, *What now?!* It sounded like the muffler was gone, so I stepped back onto the curb and looked under the car. Sure enough, it appeared that the muffler was hanging on the ground. I called a tow truck. When the driver showed up, he informed me that it was not the muffler but the catalytic converter. It had been cut off! This, he informed me, was the latest money-making scheme in Detroit.

He said that he had already picked up half a dozen cars in my neighborhood with the same problem. Damn! Here's one more thing I had to deal with. I called my husband, and he located a place for me to tow the car to. To replace the catalytic converter would be costly, so I replaced it with a straight pipe and kept moving.

Even the morning's setback didn't keep me from getting to the police station on time. But when I got there I was informed that the investigator had left for class and would be gone for a week. No, I could *not* believe it! She didn't even have the courtesy to call me. I was almost in tears. Once again, I was pressing the officer I was talking to, to find out if she had left any information for me. He snapped at me and told me in a real nasty tone of voice that she didn't. I left feeling defeated and mad as hell!

The following week the investigator got back from training and we finally met. Listening to her talk on the phone, I didn't envision her to be about fifty years old, six feet tall, about 190 pounds, and Caucasian, with gray eyes and mingled gray hair. I pictured her shorter and African American with a short haircut. As I surveyed the squad room, I saw the dingy walls and outdated equipment, and I could tell that it had seen better days. We said our pleasantries, and she immediately started telling me about her problems with her brother, who was disabled, and said that no one was helping out and everything was falling on her.

I could relate, but I needed to handle my business and get the hell on back to my husband, my home, and my life! She was telling me how heavy her workload was, trying to catch car thieves. Hell! I was trying to catch a thief too. She also told me, "I contacted Nikki and told her I wanted to talk with her, to get her side of the story, but she did not come in." I bet she didn't! While she was talking, I was thinking, *How dumb can you be! Now that you have tipped her off, she's probably in another country sitting on a sandy beach, sipping piña coladas, and spending my cousin's money!*

To make matters worse, she was asking me for the *same* documents she had requested months before! And she was still not telling me when I was going to meet with the prosecuting attorney. The ineptitude of this woman was beyond ludicrous, and I was not impressed with her. But I also was not trying to start over with someone else and have even more delays.

While I was waiting to hear about an appointment to see the prosecuting attorney, I had other things to do. Constant visits to see Aunt Helen at the nursing home, checking on May, and taking care of Mom filled my days. One Saturday afternoon, Winnye, Mom, and I stopped in to see May. While we were there, Mom constantly scratched her hands, and May yelled at her to stop. Mom denied scratching at all, which infuriated May. Before I knew it, May said, "Stop that scratching, you bitch," and then jumped out of her chair, one fist in the air, cursing (while holding on to her walker with the other hand) at Mom and yelling, "I'll beat your ass!"

Mom was not sitting still. When she heard May call her a bitch, she said, "Bitch? Who are you calling a bitch? I'll show you what a bitch I can be!" Mom jumped up from the couch, put up her fists (looking like Joe Louis), got into a fight stance, and was ready to box! And like two little kids, they were playing the dozens. If you don't know what the "dozens" means, it's simply slang for two people talking negatively about your mother, and back in the day, when I was growing up, talking about someone's mother was grounds for a fight.

Winnye and I had to jump between them to hold them back! These two women in their eighties had had a like/hate relationship for a long time. But, to actually see them in action, well, it was hilarious! We should have had film for the six o'clock news. Needless to say, I gathered up my mom, and we ended the visit and left.

Three weeks into the New Year, I was depressed, I wanted to go home, and my brain was fried. Juggling all sorts of issues, problems, and people was wearing me down, and I felt drained. I wasn't getting to the gym to exercise, and I knew that helped me get to sleep. I don't sleep well at night because my mind doesn't shut down. I was constantly listening for Mom waking up throughout the night, trying to hear what she was getting up to do, reviewing the day I had, and planning for the day(s) ahead, and when I woke up to start a new day, I was tired.

Getting enough rest is essential to staying healthy. Debbie reminded me of this one day after I told her I was short with Mom and immediately regretted it. I listened carefully to what she said: "Cyn, you need to do something to get more rest. I know you don't want to be snappish with your Mom, because that's not the normal you. And you don't want her to feel like she's a burden on you." Honestly, there were times with Mom when I just wanted to scream and run away like she did one day many years ago. I thought, *Now I understand all too well at this stage of the game what that was all about.*

I snapped back to reality when I thought about how helpless my golden girls were and that I was the only person they had to make sure they were safe and well cared for. I know my mom still looked at me like I was the child and thought who was I to tell her what to do. She demonstrated this one day when she cursed me out and raised her hand to me, because she didn't want me to tell or even ask her to do what she didn't want to do. I had to talk her down from striking me. I just wanted to be her daughter again, not a caregiver and someone she resented, even if it was only for a minute.

I retired one evening after a very busy day, and I was awakened from my sleep at about 3:30 in the morning when I heard moans coming from Mom's room. I got up to check on her, and she was holding her hand. Her fingers were curled in toward the palm of her hand, and when I attempted to straighten them, she screamed out in pain. She said it hurt too much for me to touch it. I thought back to earlier that day when she had taken a tumble from her seat while she was at the center, but she checked out fine there, came home, had her dinner using her hand, and went about her evening without a hint of discomfort.

Because it was 3:30 in the morning, I don't want to bother Wallace— he had to go to work soon. I got Mom up, got her dressed, and helped her to the car. Getting her in the car in the middle of the night in this neighborhood was a scary undertaking. Abandoned buildings and pitch-black spaces between the houses gave me the creeps.

We made it to the emergency room at Henry Ford Hospital, and that was a scary trip too. I had to pull up to the emergency room door, get Mom past the security checkpoint, watch out for the car illegally parked at the door (assuring the guard I would move it shortly), and get Mom settled in a chair. Finally I had to ask the security guard to watch out for me while I parked the car and ran through the parking lot that was several buildings away, back to the emergency room entrance. My heart was racing the whole time, and I was hoping that Mom wouldn't wonder where I was and walk away to look for me.

Mom was settled into a bed, and finally a doctor came in to speak with us. She said they would take some X-rays of Mom's hand. She asked questions, and I answered them and explained Mom's condition and the incident earlier at the center. That doctor left, and sometime later a different doctor came in.

Mom was resting in bed, and I was sitting in a chair by the bed stroking her leg when the new doctor came in. He was a young attractive African American man of medium height with a stern look on his face. Right away his posture and tone of voice put me on the defensive. He began by introducing himself and immediately went to my mother, who was awakening when he entered the room. He said to her, "Alice, please tell me how your hand got hurt." Mom looked confused and looked over to me.

"We don't really know how it got hurt," I responded.

"I was speaking to Alice," he said curtly to me.

The hair stood up on the back of my neck. I fired back, "Well, in case the information didn't trickle down to you, Doctor, my mother has Alzheimer's, and I am speaking for her!" At this point he was glaring at me, and in an utterly condescending tone he said, "I suggest you leave your mother in the hospital overnight for further observation; we're doing X-rays to determine if she has any broken bones in her hand, and I want social services to speak with her."

Who the hell did he think he was talking to? I told him, "Don't take this the wrong way, but I am not leaving my mother to wake up in a strange place alone; I am staying. And as far as social services is concerned, I am not interested in speaking to them, or at this point, Doctor, you either!" He continued trying to have a conversation with Mom and would look at me with disdain when I attempted to answer for her. What part of Alzheimer's wasn't he getting? I'm not stupid; I know he was intimating that I had to abuse my mother for her hand to be hurt.

Needless to say, we had more words. I went to the nurse's station and told the nurse standing there, "I'm requesting the supervising doctor on duty [which happened to be the first doctor] or someone else, anyone other than him. I don't like his bedside manner, and he really has upset me!" It wasn't what he said; it was the way he said it to me. I guess he didn't like that I wasn't cowering in my boots.

The first doctor came back, this time with an explanation that Mom was suffering from neuropathy (a problem with the nerve endings in her hand). She suggested Tylenol and told me that it would probably get worse. They didn't find any hairline fracture on the X-rays or anything else wrong with her hand, and I asked her if massaging would help ease the cramp in her hand. She replied, "Yes, go ahead and try that."

By the time we got back home, it was light outside, and Wallace had gone to work. I helped Mom into the house, prepared her breakfast, and made hot compresses for her hand. I also remembered the Chinese oil my friend Belinda had given me. I used it for my lower back pain, and it worked wonders for me. I rubbed the oil all over Mom's hand and continued the hot compresses for about twenty minutes. I gave her the Tylenol along with her regular medication and put her to bed. After notifying Ms. Parker what had taken place and letting her know I was keeping Mom home, I left Mom sleeping to buy her shoes that she didn't have to tie and anything else I could think of to make it easier for her to manage dressing without the use of her hand.

The next day, after I used the Chinese oil and warm compresses, Mom was up and about, her hand had straightened out, and she was ready to go back to the center. I told her she could go the next day, because I wanted to be sure that her hand was okay. She thanked me and said, "That will be fine, darling." I was more than relieved. If her hand was truly disabled, then I would have to rethink plans all around. Thankfully, it worked out fine.

In addition to all my other anxieties, I considered moving Mom and May to an assisted-living community, so I visited several and found one in Royal Oak that I thought was stellar. This facility had an impressive entrance. It looked like a Victorian home with a sweeping, grand wraparound porch. It was immaculate, with nice amenities and a daily schedule of activities. There was a backyard patio, umbrella tables and chairs, and BBQ grills. Each studio apartment was spacious and had its own mini kitchen and large bathroom, with large windows. I thought this would be a place I would live in. I left the meeting and tour with a folder of information to review. But, as nice as this place was, I was seriously conflicted about moving them.

I didn't want either of them to have to leave their homes; but I was more overwhelmed than before with trying to keep round-the-clock caregivers for May and handle all that she required. Wallace was working more overtime, which left Mom home alone for longer periods of time, and this had raised concerns for me. I needed to make a decision soon. I couldn't leave Mom to her own devices any longer. I felt more comfortable knowing that she had supervision, and her safety and security were a primary concern for me.

I didn't have the luxury of slacking off. I had to do what needed to be done, and I felt pressured to do as much as I could before I went home. There were things I could not delegate to anyone even when my friends offered to help me. What helped me immensely was talking things out with my friends.

I have wonderful friends who have been with me on this journey from the beginning and are still supporting me. They are good listeners and have provided me with invaluable insight. My daughter has suggested on numerous occasions that I should see a professional, someone neutral whom I can vent to. Yes, I considered it, but I decided my friends were better therapists than someone I didn't know and who didn't know me. I felt guilty for dominating the conversation with all my "stuff," but it's all I knew; it consumed my every waking moment and provided me with a lot of sleepless nights. I didn't have a hell of a lot of anything else going on. They told me not to worry—to get things off my chest—and I appreciated that.

Tonia, Winnye, Debbie, Lily, Barbara, Kim, Joann, Winsome, Gerry, and Peaches are the support system that breathed energy into me, and they spent many hours with me on the phone, at lunch, while I was getting my hair done, and when we were out walking, encouraging me to stay strong. I am aware that everyone may not be fortunate enough to have a family/friends support system. Caregiver support groups offer their experiences and solutions to issues that may be helpful to a seasoned caregiver or a novice.

As the weeks passed, the investigator reminded me of the Keystone Cops. I was not getting any results. In the second week of February I was really fed up and had to take matters into my own hands. I got out the phone book and found the number of the prosecuting attorney's office, Elder Abuse Department. I was prepared to get the runaround as I had been since I got there. But the first number I called was answered by a real person. I explained the reason for my call and was immediately transferred to someone else. Again, a person answered, and it was the man in charge.

I explained everything to him; it all came pouring out, and I tried not to let emotion come into play, because I felt being more professional would be more impressive. By the time I finished, he was mad, and he asked me some questions and I gave him some answers. He told me to stay close to the phone and he would call me back shortly. When we hung up, I had the feeling that he really would call me back.

True to his word, about ten minutes later he called to let me know he had spoken to the investigator and I should be receiving a call from her shortly. He told me to call him back if she didn't call me. Because President's Day was the following Monday, he told me to call him back on Tuesday and that he would have a date for us to meet. He told me that he was appalled at the way the police were dragging their feet in this case. He said he was frustrated that they did not give more importance to these cases and he had been lobbying the police department and trying to bring more attention to the crimes against elders.

He empathized with me because he also had elderly parents, and he said he would hate for something like that to happen to them. He applauded me for being an advocate for May and for coming forward. I had barely hung up from speaking to him when the phone rang again, and it was the investigator. She was very interested in helping all of a sudden. Ya think? Now it seemed she couldn't do enough for me.

The following week, I met with the head attorney and an assistant prosecuting attorney from his office. I had my file organized chronologically with all of my evidence clearly marked; this is where my professionalism and work experience paid off. I explained the situation to them concisely, and when I was done, they looked at each other and then at me, and the head attorney said to his assistant, "I told you this was a good one. We don't ever get cases this well prepared." He asked me what kind of work I did. I told him I was a retired human resources professional at a large aerospace company for twenty-two years and that I had conducted numerous investigations, testified in court, and consulted with corporate attorneys on many issues.

They took the case and issued a warrant for Nikki's arrest. Executing a warrant is the responsibility of the police, so it was back in their hands to find her and bring her in. Waiting was hard. A week went by, and I wondered if I needed to go get Nikki my damn self and turn her in. I provided the police with her address and phone number and told them where she worked and even gave them the description of her damn car! But since the investigator had called her again, who knew where she was now!

I had to turn my attention back to moving Mom and May. It was a week since I visited the assisted-living home. I was still in a state of indecision on whether I should take them there to live. It was very nice, but nice doesn't come cheap. I managed to negotiate with the home's manager a good deal on rent because I was bringing in two clients, but that still didn't solidify the deal for me.

I was in tears just thinking about it. I think I was feeling what Mom must have felt years ago, like I was committing a betrayal. I contacted the representative and told her that I just couldn't do it. The same day, while I was crying my eyes out, I got a call from May's caregiver, Benny. He told me he knew someone who was looking for work. I quickly composed myself and was very interested in what he had to say. I took down the information for this woman and immediately contacted her to set up an interview.

The woman came over to the house, and Wallace and I conducted an interview. I was thinking to myself, *Could this be a godsend?* After spending hours with her and having her in the presence of my mom, showing her around, explaining her job duties and the pay (room and board and a salary), she and I agreed to a trial stay at Mom's house.

I thought that this would give me more insight into her personality and how she interacted with Mom and handled the job overall. I explained to her that I was in the middle of some important business, but once I was done she would have the use of my room. We agreed to a two-week trial, and she went home to pack. We made up the sofa in the living room for her to sleep on.

If this worked out, Mom could stay in her home and so could May. I would continue to do the payroll and troubleshoot other issues with doctor's appointments, etc., like always. Wallace would oversee what went on in Mom's house since he was downstairs and would also continue to monitor what went on at May's house.

Wallace was wonderful with Mom, but now she needed overall care—meal preparation, housework, and more assistance with bathing and dressing—that required a woman's touch. Even though he knew he couldn't help Mom with bathing and dressing, he still felt that he had let us down, because now I had to bring someone else in to help her out. With the new setup in motion, I continued to wait for word from the police or prosecuting attorney's office.

At the beginning of March another week had passed and I was antsy. I had been away from home just about three months. I called my husband and told him that I'd had enough, to get me out of here. Apparently he was ready for me to come home too, because a short time later he e-mailed my ticket confirmation and my date to leave on March 17. My departure date still seemed far off to me. So much had happened since I got there in December; at this point I just wanted some peace and a good, sound, restful night's sleep.

For me, a little piece of heaven was not far from my mother's house—LaSalle Park. My parents used to take me there on warm summer nights when I was a child. My mom and dad would sit on the bench while I played. I also loved walking through the park on my way to and from school. It was beautiful, with its colorful fragrant flowers in the summer and wide open space glittering with untouched snow in the winter. Whenever I was in Detroit and my stress level reached maximum overload, I went to this park or Belle Isle. These places took me back to happier times, and right then, I needed to decompress badly and feel some happiness. I drove to the park and sat quietly in my car.

As I was sitting there, I received a call from the assistant prosecuting attorney. She told me that Nikki had turned herself in and was out on bail and she was working on obtaining a court date. I was beyond being relieved. Just as I was basking in this good news, the next day she called to tell me that the court date might not happen before my date to go home. She was doing her best to get the arraignment done before I had to leave but wasn't sure she could. I was on pins and needles. The next time she called and told me the date was March 18. I gladly paid $150 to change my ticket. I was ready! I had been ready!

After checking the caregivers' references and doing a background check and subjecting her to multiple interviews with various members of the family, I offered her the job of being my mother's caregiver. Before she gave me her answer, we sat down to discuss the contract and instruction guide I wrote up and asked her to review. A partial list of what I included in the contract and guidelines for "at will employment" included who was allowed in my mother's house, what her specific duties were, days off, pay periods, use of my mother's phone, use of our address to receive personal mail, contacts to call in an emergency, Mom's medical history and medical cards, schedule of medications, food allergies, etc. I did not want there to be any misunderstandings of what my expectations were, and if she had any doubt, she could check these documents or simply pick up the phone and call me. She agreed to all of my terms and conditions and signed the contract.

With the caregiver on board, I happily set that task aside and breathed a sigh of relief.

Little did I know that once again, my joy would be short-lived. I called Lily to check on her and to ask if she felt like company one day. She had been sick for some time, and I took Mom to see her as often as I could. When I called her number, an unfamiliar voice answered. I asked to speak to Lily, and I was told she was dead! I felt like I had been slapped upside my head. I told the woman that I couldn't talk right then and I would call back. I was so caught up in everything. I was dismayed that I had not called sooner. All I knew was I would miss her and our long talks and her sage advice.

Mom and Lily were very close over the years. Lily provided me with a lot of insight into what was going on with Mom during the years when I had not lived in Detroit. She also kept me abreast of important changes that needed attention in their health insurance and other things that went on with the board of education. She was a valuable asset and very instrumental in Mom's care.

A few days later, after Mom arrived home from the center, we ate dinner and I had her change into a pair of clean jeans and a blouse. I decided that I would take Mom to Lily's wake but not to the funeral. We arrived at the colonial-style funeral home with its enormous flower urns on the front porch. We found Lily's suite; it was decorated with Queen Anne furnishings and heavy drapery. The room was already crowded with her family when we got there. When we approached the casket, Mom asked, "Cyn, is that really Lily lying there?"

"Yes, honey, it's really her," I said.

She stood quietly for a few minutes and then moved on to greet Lily's niece and nephew. When she spoke to the nephew, she tried to fall out on the floor, howling like she was cut or something. Now all eyes were on Mom. Someone brought her some water and helped her to a chair. She wept (but there were no tears) and moaned. I finally decided to take her out of the building, and she howled all the way out the door.

But as soon as we hit the sidewalk and there was no audience, the howling stopped! I told her, "Girl, you know you ought to stop." I decided to take her for a ride to take her mind off of the wake. I said, "Come on, Mom; let's go for a ride to Belle Isle, and I will buy you a hot dog and a pop." She beat me to the car. As we were driving along, I asked her, "Mom, are you going to miss Lily?" and just that quickly, she responded, "Lily? Why? Is she going somewhere?" She didn't even remember that Lily was dead. Wallace and I attended Lily's funeral services and said our good-byes. She was a good friend to my mom, Wallace, and me, and I miss her. Lily, rest in peace.

Three long months had passed, and my day in court finally arrived. I had May and Benny with me along with Ms. Karla Cole and a representative from the Comerica bank to testify. After I gave my testimony, I was free to go home. Because every word I said was recorded, there was no need for me to be present at the next court hearing. It was all about the prosecutor from there on out. I had the utmost confidence in this young prosecuting attorney. She was a pit bull in a skirt, and she gave Nikki's attorney a royal beating during the hearing I attended. There was no reason for me to believe that she would not do the same thing if Nikki was bound over for trial. You go, girl! I left for home on March 23 and was very happy that everything I worked hard to accomplish had finally fallen into place.

Once I got home, I fell into the routine of calling every day to speak with my mother and her caregiver to see how things were going with them. Things seemed to be going well; so far no complaints from anyone. Even though I was home, my work wasn't done. I sifted through all the paperwork I accumulated while I was in Detroit, sorting, shredding, and filing what I brought home and in some instances following up on issues that were not completed before I left there. I can't even remember how I handled a job and still did what needed to be done for them without drinking myself into a coma. After retiring, the workload increased, and it became pretty much a full-time job. The paperwork associated with these four women (even though Aunt Margaret passed in 2007, I was still trying to settle unresolved issues on her behalf) plus my own personal business was astronomical.

The prosecutor called me at home to tell me that the judge bound Nikki over for trial and they had a hearing date. Now I was really joyful. At our initial meeting the prosecutors asked me what I hoped to achieve by prosecuting Nikki and if my goal was to see her in jail. I told them, "Hell no. I don't want her in jail. I want her to pay back my cousin's money. I don't care if she has to sell her body, her house, or that Mercedes she drives! I want the money!" I said, "Tell her to draw the money down from her retirement or 401k plans. If she can't do that, then teach her a lesson, and put her under the jail."

What was disappointing was that I could only sue for the money I could prove she took beyond a shadow of a doubt. At this point, I'd take it, because $9,000 was a significant amount of money to an elderly person living on a pension. The hearing took place, and the judge ruled that Nikki must repay the money. Additionally, the prosecutor's office wanted a piece of the action too, so they imposed a five-year probation period on her.

The prosecutor called to tell me that she had Nikki's check. My husband was in Detroit on business, and he picked up the check and deposited the money in May's account the same day. Victory! Oh, I was so ecstatic! Now that the theft drama was over, I had to get back to work on the fiduciary accounting for the court, which was due soon. I absolutely dreaded having to go through this process because documentation was not in order; even so, I had to do what I could. In the midst of preparing the report for the court, I decided to see if I could actually bring my dream back to life.

The previous year, I got my business license, state tax identification number, business cards, and a phone number. I advertised and had a marketing plan to put my name out there, but a year later nothing was happening. In the scheme of things, if a person or family is on a budget, the last thing they have money to spend on is interior decorating and a designer to do it. In spite of all my efforts to bring in business, I did not generate any interest. I wanted to believe it was largely due to the economy. Who was I kidding? My numerous trips to Detroit didn't leave me a lot of time or energy to put into a business the way I should.

I felt defeated as I looked around my office at my diplomas and certificates, and I decided to call Detroit and talk to Debbie. I told her how I felt and that I had contemplated throwing in the towel on my design business.

Debbie said to me, "Interior design may be the career you chose, but I think that writing a book is what's going to eventually choose you. Writing about all you've been through may be what you really need to do, Cyn. Lots of people will benefit from it because just being with you and seeing all that you've been through has helped me with my dad. You may not be able to see it now, but you should seriously think about writing a book." It's this kind of encouragement from Debbie and Winnye and others that started me on the path of thinking about writing this book even at this stage of the game. So I closed the door on my business.

I had been home two months, and things were beginning to change in Detroit. Wallace was telling me that the caregiver had already broken one of the conditions of her employment by having people in my mother's house without prior permission from me. When I addressed this with her, she seemed a little irate that I was even speaking to her about it. I was also playing mediator between her and Wallace, who were both acting like children. After her explanation, I allowed it to pass and gave her a second chance.

One day I called Mom to see how things were going, and I could not get through. The phone just kept ringing, and the voice mail would not pick up. After I could not reach them on the housephone (and Wallace was at work, not answering his phone), I called the caregiver's cell phone. She informed me that "everything is fine now." I asked her to elaborate on what that meant.

She explained, "Well, last night sometime around 4:00 a.m. I heard noises in the alley behind the house. I got out of bed and went to the window and saw flames engulfing a neighbor's garage, across the alley from your mom's house. The sight of the fire was frightening, but I kept cool, immediately got dressed first, called Wallace, and got your mom dressed and out of the house. A short time later, the fire department arrived and put out the fire. But the fire damaged telephone lines and the streetlight that was there." The telephone service was out for almost a week before the phone company was able to restore service to the house. Meanwhile, I called the caregiver's cell phone to speak to Mom.

After I hired the caregiver, I introduced her to Ms. Parker and asked that Ms. Parker monitor Mom's behavior and check her out when she came to the center to make sure she was not physically harmed in any way. I used this as another measure of insurance to make sure Mom was being treated well. But even with Wallace downstairs and Ms. Parker looking out for her, when I called home now, I was beginning to hear a change in my mother's voice. Her tone had changed, and the caregiver seemed more belligerent at times. When she called my mother to pick up the phone, her tone of voice was harsh.

On several occasions when I called, my mom was in her room with the door locked and was whispering into the phone. It was on one of these occasions that the hair stood up on the back of my neck, so I booked a flight to Detroit the same day. It was my gut telling me that it was time to go home.

I spoke with Wallace one day and asked him if he was seeing any changes in Mom. That's when he informed me, "I've been working late, and by the time I get home, she is already in bed. I don't want to disturb your mom or the caregiver. That babysitter from hell gets on my nerves, and I don't want to be around her." I blew my stack! Expletives flew out of my mouth, like I was possessed by ten sailors.

I believe this was the first time I had ever lost my temper with Wallace. I yelled at him, "Wallace, this is not about you; it's about Momma! How the hell are you letting someone else control your house? You're the man of the house! And you're letting this woman come into your house and punk you? What's wrong with you? You can go anywhere in that house any time you feel like it. You have always assured me that you would take care of Mom, and I expected you to be there to check on her like you were supposed to no matter who or what!"

I continued. "Wallace, you must be kidding me!" I shouted at him, "That woman could be doing something to Mom, and since you aren't checking on her, Mom wouldn't even have the chance to tell you if she was being mistreated. So get upstairs and check on my mother!" He said, "You're right, sis. I'll go upstairs and check things out when we get off the phone."

Because of the bad blood between Wallace and the caregiver I didn't tell him I was coming. I didn't want him to accidentally tip her off. And I also knew he would love to antagonize her with that kind of information.

I arrived in Detroit on Thursday, July 8. Debbie picked me up at the airport, and we arrived at Mom's house, a two-family flat with big porches upstairs and down, at about 8:30 p.m. I carried my luggage from the car to the front porch and opened the door into the downstairs hall. I heard the caregiver asking who was there. I identified myself and proceeded upstairs to put down one of my suitcases in the living room, gave my mom a hug, and returned to the front porch to get the rest of my luggage. By this time Wallace had come to the front door of his flat and we spoke briefly.

The next thing I know, Mom was downstairs on the front porch in her pants, T-shirt, and bare feet, with her tennis shoes in her hand. "I'm ready, Cyn; let's go."

I told her, "Honey, I'm here to visit you for a while, so we can have some fun." But she just kept saying she was ready to go as she looked over her shoulder.

Debbie left, and Mom and I went in the house and back upstairs. The house was immaculately clean, and I sat down with the caregiver and asked her how she was doing and how things were going. She said things were fine and wanted to know how I was doing. We continued with polite conversation for a while until she finally left the room and returned to what she was doing in the kitchen when I came in. It was extremely hot in the house and very uncomfortable. I could feel tension in the air. I noticed that Mom seemed meek when the caregiver was in the room and was constantly giving her compliments, as someone would do to a bully to stay on their good side. I was watching very closely everything around me.

After Mom and I visited for a while, the caregiver assisted Mom in getting ready for bed. Since I relinquished my room to the caregiver, I had to sleep in the living room on the sofa. It was so hot that there was no possible way I would sleep. Besides the heat, I decided that it was best if I kept one eye open.

Friday morning, the caregiver got Mom up and bathed, dressed, and fed her, and she was ready to get on the van and go to the center. I was heartbroken that my mother didn't even remember that I was in the house (not something that she just started, but something I had not adapted to). After Mom left, I asked the caregiver to sit down so we could talk. The expression on her face indicated that she was concerned. She asked me if she had done something wrong, and I told her that I was disappointed that she did not adhere to the contract she signed and that she had broken some of those rules and seemed to take them lightly.

I told her that I was taking over because my mother should be with me. I gave her notice that as of that day, she was relieved of her duties, that I would take care of my mother while she made preparations for other living arrangements. I paid her and gave her two weeks' notice in writing to move out; but I told her if she could go sooner, I would make it worthwhile. She said she would be gone by Saturday afternoon. I reclaimed my mother's house and my mother without incident.

When Mom returned home from the center that evening she had no reaction to the caregiver's absence. We went about doing what we always did when I was there, and she was out of her room again and free to live in her entire house. Wallace came up and ate dinner with us. Thankfully, Mom was not physically harmed, and I hugged and kissed her more now than ever to let her know she was not alone.

After the caregiver left that Saturday, I cleaned my room thoroughly, called the plumber to fix a clogged drain to alleviate water that was backing up into the basement, and called the locksmith to change all the locks the first thing Monday.

On Tuesday, I met with a representative from the assisted-living home I had visited in February. The experience with the live-in caregiver fortified me to do what I felt had to be done; my concern more than ever was about Mom's safety. Mom could no longer be in the house alone. And at May's house, trying to keep round-the-clock caregivers and running a household from afar was draining me.

With two clients that I could use as leverage, I negotiated a lower rent for Mom and May and locked the rate in for a year. Looking back now, I would not do that again—month to month is better, because you may need to move them before the year is up. (Of course there are escape clauses for certain situations.) The next thing was getting all the paperwork done, medical examinations for both, and packing up May's household.

Moving them to assisted living felt right to me this time, for several reasons. This home was run by a big corporation, and I would have recourse here if something bad happened. There were multiple layers of management, and everyone was watching everyone. Written documentation (e.g., medical charts, billing statements, incident reports, etc.) was available for review if necessary.

And the facility was all-inclusive, which meant that there were daily activities, movies, crafts, and road trips too. The dining room was restaurant quality with tablecloths and fine china. Overall it was a top-notch facility. The one thing I regretted was that I would not be able to let Mom continue to go to the center, because it was not close to the assisted-living home.

I turned my attention to May's house. It was in disrepair, and it would have taken a big chunk of her money to repair it to try to rent it, like I did for Aunt Helen. I knew I would not get the kind of rent I needed to offset May's expenses and I was not likely to get the type of renter I desired to rent in this neighborhood. Besides that, I did not want to be or have the patience to be an absentee landlord. That was a very scary proposition to undertake in the city of Detroit. I wasn't looking forward to dismantling another household of more than fifty years either, but May's house did not hold any sentiment for me like Aunt Helen's.

I was exhausted before I even got started with this move. I was going about organizing my plan to accomplish all the tasks associated with moving not one but two people. Normal chores still had to be done as well, like laundry, grocery shopping, cooking, housework, etc. Plus I still had to see about Aunt Helen. Winnye said, "Girl, you make my head spin with all the things you handle when you're here; I think I should call you the 'Pink Power Ranger.'"

We laughed and I told her, "I love spending time with my mom, but I'm motivated to get back home; it seems like I spend more time here than I do there."

On Sunday night it was extremely hot outside and inside the house. I had the front and back doors open to get any breeze that might be moving around. I was in my room watching television, and Mom was in the dining room watching *The Godfather*. Wallace was downstairs watching *The Godfather* too. I was in my room sweating bullets, so I walked to the front porch door, only to find that it was closed, and when I checked, so was the back door. I asked Mom not to close the doors so we could get a breeze. As I opened the back door again, it dawned on me that it was pitch black in the alley and backyard, and it gave me a creepy feeling; goose bumps ran down my arms. The streetlight in the alley had not been repaired since the fire. Once again, I went to the front and the door was closed.

Once more I said to Mom, "Honey, don't close the doors. Just leave them open for now. I'll lock up before I go to bed." She never stopped looking at the television as I walked by, and she said to me, "You better watch out or something's gonna get'cha." I stopped in my tracks, because the way she said it creeped me out to the point that the hair stood up on the back of my neck. Trust and believe that I quickly closed the back door, because now it felt like someone was watching us, and the neighborhood had become eerily quiet.

By the following week, other things that the caregiver did began to come to light, like her giving out my mother's phone number. (People were calling like this was her house.) Her contract stated that she was supposed to use her own telephone number. She also used my mother's address (her packages were being delivered here) when her contract stated that she was to receive mail at a post office box or another place of her choosing.

These were things that violated her contract that she blatantly lied about when I asked her about them. As she was moving out that Saturday, her son was helping her move; he let it slip that he had been in the house on several occasions. Again, her contract stated that she was not to have visitors without my prior knowledge and approval. Busted! I knew she was up to something, because when I called one day she was trying to rush me off the phone and hurry my conversation with Mom. But after I talked to Mom and she got back on the phone to talk to me, before she could hang up, I heard her visitors talking in the background.

Yep. And as if that wasn't enough, later on I found out the reason she wasn't answering my calls was because she was on the housephone for hours on some 800 line. The moment I left town, she started taking over and doing what she wanted to do. What a bonus for her, when Wallace stopped coming up as often as he used to, to check on things. Good riddance! Moving forward!

After all the drama, I decided that Mom and I should go out on a date. It was Saturday and she didn't have to go to the center, so I suggested that we go to a movie and have dinner afterward. She was excited, and we headed off to the movies. Since going to the center was going so well, Mom thought she was supposed to go somewhere seven days a week. I was happy to see her more active and raring to go (a far better improvement on her sitting around tearing up sale papers all day).

When the movie was over, we went to a restaurant nearby and were seated in a booth. The waitress left the menus and walked away. The little momma was sneaky: she had her menu in front of her, hiding her face while she was inching her hand across the table to take the sugar, ketchup, and mustard packets, and she was shoving them in her pockets, as if I couldn't see her. I gave up on getting her to stop that long ago. It only made her mad at me, and it frustrated me.

Actually it was kind of funny. For instance, Mom would come in from the center every day and her shirt would be bumpy and lumpy. When I asked her, "Mom, what's going on up here in your bra?" she would push my hand away and tell me, "Girl, leave me alone." I stuck my hand in her shirt and pulled out plastic cutlery, paper cups, tissue, and cookies! I thought the next thing that might come out of there was a Volkswagen with ten people in it. She even had to laugh. We've always called her generous bosom "the vault," and she certainly was keeping her stash of goodies safe down in there.

Mom was hoarding and hiding things more often now. I noticed that as her Alzheimer's progressed, she began to feel that she never had enough of everything. She had a tendency to hoard facial tissue and toilet paper. It became a problem because she hid it all over the house (under her bed, in the closet, in dresser drawers, and in her clothing). If I neglected to check her pockets and sleeves, it would be on *everything* in the washer and dryer; what a mess.

On Monday the nineteenth, I went to the grocery store to pick up a few things for the house. I returned home and was about to get out of the car when a song I liked played on the radio. As I sat there listening to the song and thinking about all that had happened over the years, I began to cry uncontrollably. When the song was over, I continued to sit in front of the house a while longer to compose myself. I finally got out of the car and took the groceries in the house. As I was putting them away, I realized how hot it was in the house, and I went to the back door in the kitchen to open the upstairs back porch door (which is located outside the kitchen, off a short hall).

As I was doing this, I noticed a light coming from around the corner and down the back stairs leading to the downstairs back porch door. At first I thought, *I must have left the light on down there.* No, there was no light at the bottom of the stairs, only at the top of the stairs. So I cautiously made my way to the corner of the first stairwell landing and saw that the downstairs back porch door was standing wide open! I immediately eased back up the stairs and into the kitchen (I had no idea if there might be someone behind me in the attic) and slammed the door and ran downstairs to the front porch and called 911!

The 911 number was busy! I couldn't believe it! No, this was no joke. Detroit has had a lot of financial troubles over the years and has had quite a few cutbacks. I kept dialing and still could not get through. I called my friend Joann (she lives in a suburb of Detroit) and told her what was going on, and she called 911 from her house to see if her 911 operator could get through.

I thought, *What if they got into Wallace's house?* I looked through the windows and did not see anything out of place. While Joann was calling 911, I went into the backyard and went up on the porch to get a closer look at the door, just to make sure it had not been left open and the wind blew it open. But that couldn't happen. We have a heavy iron security door protecting the interior door. No, the frame of the door was shattered. As I stood there it dawned on me that the thief could still be in the basement, so I quickly locked the basement door and ran back to the front of the house.

I waited at least forty minutes before the police showed up. Damn, I needed them to get there to see what was happening before the van pulled up to bring Mom home from the center. Two police officers finally responded, and we went through the house checking the upstairs rooms and closets. They went into the attic, and we all went into the basement and up into Wallace's house.

That's where the damage was done. Wallace's televisions were gone! Nothing else in the house had been touched. He had the newer flat screens (easy-to-carry models). I contacted Wallace at work, and he came home. The officers determined that whoever robbed the house knew the lay of the land, because it would not be apparent to a stranger that the basement had no wall separating the two sides of the basement. Wallace immediately accused the caregiver whom he referred to as the babysitter from hell!

I had to admit that she was a prime suspect in my mind too, but I could not overlook the fact that the Saturday before this happened, the plumber and his two helpers were in the basement. It was easy for them to spot the boxes that the televisions came in as they were still in the basement. And I wasn't down there with them the whole time, because they had me running up and down the stairs turning the water on and off in the kitchen. It would have been easy for one of them to case the other side and see that the door leading from the basement into his house was not locked.

The caregiver had carte blanche to the house daily (except for Wallace's days off). She could have easily gone through to the other side of the basement and up in to Wallace's house (because he did not install the lock I left him for that door when I decorated the flat), looked around at everything he had, and filed that information away. I also could have left the door unlocked after walking the plumber to his truck that day and forgotten to go back and lock it. But even with that, someone would have to know to check the security door and the back door to find that they were unlocked.

And someone would have to know that even though there was a dog bowl on the back porch, there was no dog. These unanswered questions gave me pause and cause to have reasonable doubt in my mind about one or the other. The bottom line was that we would never know.

After the theft, because I felt that it could have been my fault, I replaced Wallace's televisions and insisted that he get renters' insurance, because if it happened again, it would be on him to replace anything stolen. With this latest drama over, I attempted to put my head on straight again and get over the feeling of being violated. I had too much work to do, and I wanted to get home.

I discussed moving Mom to the assisted-living home with Darryl, Tonia, and Wallace (and practically anyone else who would listen). I needed more reassurance that I was doing the right thing. I got mixed reviews, but ultimately the decision rested with me. I decided to go through with it, and I set up their doctors' appointments and completed the paperwork required by the home. I also needed to break the news to Ms. Parker at the center. She actually took it pretty well, but I had the feeling that she didn't believe me at first. She asked, "Where is your mom going? I'll be happy to check on her sometimes," and there was never any doubt in my mind that she wouldn't. She had never let me down before.

Now that the decision has been made to move Mom and May, it created another dilemma for me to think about and resolve. I was concerned about the house being empty upstairs and downstairs with Wallace working so much. Empty houses in Detroit are magnets for thieves to gut them and take everything out, nailed down or not. Furnaces, water heaters, air conditioners, copper piping, fixtures of any kind—if anything has some value to it, they take it.

My solution to making the house look occupied was timers that attached to the lights, appliances, and televisions. However, my concerns about making the house look occupied were soon allayed when my sister-in-law Barbara called to say she would rent Mom's flat and she wanted to move in next month. Cool! Problem solved.

July 29 was the day I moved Mom and May to the assisted-living home. May's primary caregiver, Benny, and I coordinated to get them to the doctor's appointment and from there directly to the assisted-living home. Once there, we escorted them to their studio apartments; this was a large studio with a nice-sized living area, private bathroom, small refrigerator, counter with sink, upper and lower cabinets, a dining table, and two closets, and each room had big windows with outside light and a view. They were already furnished (using the home's furniture). I opted to use the home's furniture so I could move quickly. I selected a few pieces from Mom's and May's homes and integrated those pieces into their new apartments to help them feel connected to their new environment. I selected apartments that were adjacent to each other (so Mom and May could be close and know that family was near), and they were located just a few feet from the nurse's station.

After they were moved in, when it was time to go, it was one of the hardest things I had ever done in my life. I felt so guilty, just like

I did whenever I left Tonia at the babysitter's and she would cry. I went home and cried like a baby. The house felt odd without Mom there. I told myself that I had tried every option open to me and this was the best thing for both of them and maybe me too. I could not care for them the way they needed to be cared for, I had to listen to the same advice I had given Mom years before. I had to realize that it was time to let go.

The assisted-living home's nurse said, "I want you to stay away for a few days so the staff can get to know them and they can acclimate to their new surroundings." In prior meetings with management, I had already warned them that Mom and May could be like water and oil and that May's personality was not conducive to getting along with people. Mom, on the other hand, would overall be personable and cheerful but could be stubborn when she didn't want to do something.

Not even twenty-four hours passed before the home called and informed me that the girls were fussing, cussing, and trying to fight! May was fussing at Mom because she was in her room and took her pictures. (They both had similar pictures of family members.) After the three days were up, I began to visit daily and saw that they seemed to be adjusting, although I would have to sneak away when Mom wasn't looking to keep her from trying to leave with me.

The staff took my advice and seated them at separate tables in the dining room, and that helped to keep the peace. Mom was active in everything they offered. May didn't want to participate in anything; she just sat in her room in the dark. Not too surprising or out of character for her, because this was pretty much what she did in her own home.

I called the real estate agent who had listed Aunt Helen's house and signed the papers to list May's house in August. I was hoping this house would sell quickly. Wallace, the real estate agent, and May's neighbors were diligent about keeping an eye on her property to keep it from being vandalized.

Every trip I made to Detroit kept me running between visits to Mom and May and Aunt Helen at the nursing home. Aunt Helen's health was in limbo. She was wheelchair bound and without the benefit of activity, so she had also gained weight. Her attendant got her out of bed daily so she could sit and eat her meals with the other residents. Her speech was almost indiscernible, but sometimes she responded with her eyes and occasionally surprised me with a coherent comment.

On one such occasion, when I walked into her room and bent over to kiss her, she said very clearly, "I like your coat. You smell good." I was so happy. I kissed her more and tried to keep her talking. But the moment passed as quickly as it had come. I never assumed that because she had Alzheimer's she would not understand what I was saying to her. I spoke to her normally and hoped that something I said would resonate with her and that she knew I was there for her.

A few days before I left for home, Aunt Helen was sent to Sinai Grace Hospital because she was having involuntary seizures. By the time I was notified and Wallace and I rushed over to the hospital, I was told that she had been discharged back to the nursing home. I was not happy about having made a wasted trip, but when we got to the nursing home, Aunt Helen was alert and sitting in her wheelchair. I told her it was time for me to go back to California and she nodded her head as though she understood what I was saying. I kissed her, told her I loved her, and said good-bye.

Being in Mom's house without her really depressed me; I felt my spirit fall to depths it had never been before. Even though I visited her daily, I missed her not being at home. I left Detroit for home and rejuvenation on August 16. After a few weeks of being at home, I got a call from the assisted-living home's nurse. She seemed a little anxious when she called to talk to me. She began by telling me of other incidents May had with my mother and that they had been close to blows and the attendants had to separate them. She asked for permission to move one of them to the first floor. I was very receptive to this idea, but I explained to her that I was not in town and would have to try to round up family and friends to move her belongings. She told me not to worry, that they would be more than happy to take care of it, and they did. Problem solved.

One problem solved is a blessing; when two are resolved, I am more than joyful. My fiduciary hearing was also in August. Back in June my attorney told me that, as expected, the fiduciary report did not balance. We never got it to balance, and at the court hearing, the attorneys agreed that the court should allow the report due to the prior mismanagement of funds. To support this decision, as promised, the prosecuting attorney's office wrote a letter on my behalf to the judge explaining my efforts in pursuing the return of May's money. The judge approved the accounting. I breathed a sigh of relief, as I could now move on to other issues that needed my attention.

The assisted-living home was beautiful and very expensive, and I could see that I would need to find additional funding if Mom and May were going to stay there. I found out through the assisted-living home that spouses married to veterans who were now themselves disabled might be entitled to spousal benefits, but you had to apply for them. Although May was not eligible at this stage (she did not meet the financial limitation), I knew that at some point, especially paying the expenses in the assisted-living home, she would need it. After reading through the Department of Veterans Affairs (VA) application, I discovered that even though May's husband was a Korean War veteran, that was not the only criterion she needed to meet to receive the benefit.

Veterans Service Organizations (VSO—check the VA website for a local listing) can assist you in completing an application and advise you on what supporting documentation is needed, at no charge. I chose to complete the application myself for the *Dependency and Indemnity Compensation, Death Pension and Accrued Benefits by a Surviving Spouse or Child (Including Death Compensation if Applicable)* (VA Form 21-534). And in addition to this form, I also completed the *Social Security Administration Application for Survivor's Benefits* (Form SSA-24). This form is optional but recommended by the VA. I completed everything on my own and then hand-delivered it to the VSO on November 9, 2010.

I sat down with a representative and asked him to review my application to ensure that I had not missed anything, because I didn't want them to have any reason to delay their approval. He made a few minor modifications, and I was told that it could take as much as six months to a year to get a determination. A few weeks later, I received a letter from the VA telling me they had the application in St. Paul, Minnesota, and to be patient; they were processing my request.

Darryl's father was not doing well, and his health was failing rapidly since Darryl had seen him in October. After Darryl returned home from Alabama, we tried to have a happy Thanksgiving, but our mood was very sullen. Darryl insisted that we put up our Christmas tree to try to lighten our mood, but a few days after we did that, he received a call from his sister Barbara, who was in Alabama with their dad, telling him that we should get there as soon as possible, because the doctors did not give him much time. We packed our RV and left immediately, but he passed away before we got there. We arrived in Alabama and began preparations to bury him. Pops, rest in peace.

After the funeral, Darryl and I left for Georgia in our RV to spend time with my dad, Myrna, and Tonia. When we arrived on Christmas Eve, the weather was extremely cold. The next day, we woke up to a winter wonderland. (We were parked in a national historical park, with Bambi running through the woods.) The news reported that this snowfall was the first one Georgians had seen in one hundred years.

We enjoyed Christmas day with my family opening gifts, eating dinner, and having a good time. The next day, we prepared to hit the road for home; we found that hoses on the RV were frozen so stiff that we had to use a blow dryer to thaw them; oh yes, this was a new camping experience for us.

The trip home was somewhat somber, but the weather continually improved as we drove farther west, and that helped to lift our spirits. We arrived home December 30 and proceeded to unpack the RV, take down the Christmas tree, clean our house, and wash clothes in preparation for New Year's Eve. After all the cleaning and washing off the road grime, the next day we settled in for the evening to enjoy our home and ring in the New Year. We opened a bottle of champagne and toasted ourselves, friends, family, and the upcoming New Year.

## 2011

In February, I contacted the VA to get a status on my application. I was informed that they required additional information from me because the court documents (guardian/conservator papers) were unacceptable and they needed May to sign everything they send. I could not sign on her behalf, so everything I signed for her had to be redone. I needed to have May complete an *Authorization to Disclose Personal Information to a Third Party* (Form 21-0845). Huh? This means that the VA wouldn't discuss the claim with me without this form.

They also requested a *Statement in Support of Claim* (Form 21-4138.) This form was needed to tell the VA why she thought she was entitled to the benefits. Come on. Can you say *Alzheimer's!* I asked the representative how she was supposed to sign something that she didn't understand. She had Alzheimer's—therefore the term "incapacitated individual." She explained to me that if May could in any way sign her name or make her X they wanted her to do it. This didn't make any sense to me.

Wallace took a friend with him, and they witnessed May sign her name. Oh and by the way, they also required us to put her thumbprint on a sheet of paper for further identification. I had to be on the phone coaching her to sign, and she complied without too much hassle. Whew! Little did I know that this was just the beginning of my frustration and how taxing this process would be on my patience.

In March it was time for me to prepare for another trip to Detroit; there was finally an offer on May's house, and we were going into escrow. But before I can finalize the sale, I must petition the court for permission to sell it. So on April 13 I appeared before the judge and he approved the sale. The escrow closed on April 19. I also sold her car the very next day, a few hours before leaving for the airport to return home. Everything went right down to the wire, but I was finally able to close the book on that chapter of May's life. I felt like another huge burden had been lifted from my shoulders, and I was relieved not to have those responsibilities and the expenses of maintaining a household any more.

The months passed quickly. It was almost May again and time for me to begin preparing the second fiduciary accounting (which covered May 7, 2010, through May 6, 2011). These accountings would continue each year until May no longer had any assets, real or monetary. The attorney appointed this year was proving to be very tenacious and aggressive, and my attorney seemed intimidated by him. I worked on the suggestions he made to get the account to balance and was once again praying that it would balance and I could be done with it.

Mom and May moved into their assisted-living home in 2010, and their lease expired at the end of July 2011. As nice as it was, I couldn't afford for them to continue to stay there any longer, and I needed to get back there and find other accommodations for them. But before I did that, I wanted to go see Tonia.

My daughter was graduating from the University of Phoenix with her doctorate in organizational leadership, and I was very proud of her! She is very smart, with a BA, two master's degrees, and now her doctorate. She was the first member of our branch of the family to achieve such a high degree of education. I was going to the graduation ceremony held in Georgia, and I was looking forward to spending time with her, Daddy, and Myrna. We enjoyed doing girlie things like pedicures and going shopping and to lunch. We even went to her belly-dancing class, and that was a blast! After an hour of gyrating and bust-popping moves, I was soaking wet! It felt good to let my hair down and actually have some fun.

After the graduation ceremony, Tonia held a meet and greet for her friends and family to celebrate her achievement. A few days later, it was time for me to pack for the next leg of my trip. I left Georgia and headed to Detroit on June 29. I arrived at my mother's house in the late afternoon to find Wallace chilling on the front porch. He immediately dropped a bomb on me that our next door neighbor wanted me to remove a tree that had fallen in his yard during a recent storm.

Why was I just now hearing about it? Can't I even get my luggage in the house before I have to *do* something! Damn! I don't think I will ever get used to coming into town and hitting the ground running. Literally once I was there, it was nonstop running around. This tree removal was just another blip on the screen of things to do. I made arrangements for the tree to be cut up and hauled away the next day. Before I could recover from news about the tree, he dropped a bigger bomb on me that he was sick, really sick! Oh my God, I was physically ill. I was stunned … Please Lord, not Wallace.

He had scheduled doctors' appointments for tests the following week. Barbara and I agreed that we needed to be with him for those appointments. We shared Mom's upstairs flat when I was in town. She and I discussed what a blessing it was for her to be in the house with him and help him out when he needed it. It just goes to show that you never know how the Lord will work things out for you.

On Monday, I began researching other places for Mom and May to stay. While I was in California, I looked into a few assisted-living homes that were in my neighborhood and found out they were called "room and board" homes. They were literally houses (not commercial buildings) that the owners have converted into facilities for the disabled and/or mentally challenged. They provided some of the same services the assisted-living homes did, except for less money and usually not on tiers like the assisted-living homes.

When I started my search in Detroit, I was looking for "room and board" homes and was not finding any. Through a few phone calls and networking with my friends, I found out that in Michigan these places are referred to as "adult foster care" (AFC) homes. Who knew? Now that I had the correct terminology, I went online to the State of Michigan Department of Human Services website and hit the jackpot. There were hundreds of them all over the inner city and suburbs.

My online research revealed that before a home owner could open their doors to the public, the state of Michigan sends an inspector to these homes to ensure that they have all the state-required qualifications needed to open the home. After they are approved, the inspector makes subsequent random visits to ensure that the homes are continually up to state standards, rules, and regulations.

The actual reports filed by the home owner and the inspector are also available for viewing. These reports tell you how big the residence is, how many residents it will accommodate, the square footage, what kind of services are provided and for what kind of client, and more. They also include any grievances filed by the residents and/or their caregivers and the resolutions to those complaints, which are part of the home owner's record. When you choose a home that you are interested in viewing, all this information is at your fingertips. I found it very comprehensive and extremely helpful. After reading this information on each of the homes I wanted to see, I was able to hone my list and save myself some time.

I made a list of homes in the locations I wanted to see and then sorted through them by the services they provided. (I was specifically looking for places that catered to dementia/Alzheimer's clients.) After I narrowed the list to twelve homes, I made appointments to visit and tour each one, until I found one that met my expectations of cleanliness, services, and price. Another important thing to consider is how you interact with the home's owner.

I found a home called Autumn Ravines, in Southfield, that offered a private room that I was interested in for Mom. But the private rooms were more than May could afford, so I decided that since May had a hard time getting along with Mom, this would be a good time to separate them. I really didn't want to separate them, because it just made another trip to another location for me to travel to. There was another place on my list that I had in mind for May and even though it was only three miles from where Mom would be living, it would add to my stress to have to manage yet another facility. And on top of that, I had to consider friends who were willing to assist me. I didn't want them running all over town either. Even though my friends had been extraordinary with their support, I certainly didn't want them burned out.

Everything was arranged for Mom to move into Autumn Ravines, but I still had to find and secure a place for May. The owner of the first home I was interested in for May agreed to meet with May and me at the assisted-living home so she could assess May's disability and decide if she was a candidate for her services and her home. The woman seemed capable, and her qualifications on paper seemed very good. She owned more than one home and had been referred to me by my friend's friend. I told her that I was trying to coordinate moving them by or before the end of their lease on July 29. She stated she had a semiprivate room available that May could share with a ninety-year-old woman. She invited me to stop by and see the house and let her know if I wanted the room. I explained to her I had just begun my search and had a few more homes to see. I told her I would make my decision by the middle of the week.

I called her on Wednesday to tell her I had seen the house, I wanted the room, and I would be willing to stop by and leave a good faith deposit to let her know that I was serious about the rental. I did that on Thursday, leaving the check and instructions with her house manager to hold the check until May moved in.

The following week, I contacted the owner to ask how much rent I would need to move May in. I was told that I needed to pay more than I expected. We disagreed on the amount. Because I was moving May in during the middle of the month, I told her that the rent should be pro-rated for that month. She told me I needed to pay for the entire month, plus the deposit. I thought, *Is she crazy or what? Am I missing something?* And I was taken aback by the tone of voice and the manner in which she was speaking to me. My radar went up, and I had to step back and think. Perhaps she was having a bad day; that was on Monday. The next day, my gut told me that something wasn't right. Here I was the client, and she was talking to me like I had a tail. How would she treat May when I was gone? I called my bank to put a stop payment on the check and was not surprised when the bank representative informed me that the check I had asked them to hold had been cashed.

I immediately got on the phone and called her to ask her about cashing the check she was supposed to hold, and things got ugly.

She screamed at me, telling me, "Once you gave me the check it was mine to do with what I wanted." What! Are you nuts! I was thinking this chick had lost her mind. If you know anything about me, you would know that I am not the one to mess with, especially when it came to my golden girls and their money.

I listened to her and then calmly asked, "Please explain to me how in the world you think you are entitled to cash the check when you have not provided any services, May has not moved in, and there is no signed contract?" I continued. "You obviously made a bad decision in cashing my check. I will be at the house at 1:00 p.m. today to pick up my money. Please make sure that it is there when I arrive."

She calmed down a bit and asked, "Listen, you're right. I apologize. Can we start over? I've been under some stress lately, and I didn't mean to be curt with you. I'll agree that you can pay what you want to pay." I responded, "I might be inclined to allow you a second chance if I was dealing with my money and if I was only dealing with me and not someone I loved. Therefore, I must decline to continue any relationship with you. At this point I just want my money by 1:00 p.m., and *please* don't disappoint me." Wallace and I showed up at the home on time and found that the check was waiting. I promptly drove to her bank and recovered May's money.

Everything happens for a reason, and this obviously was not the place for May to be. I returned to Autumn Ravines, and the owner informed me he had rented the other room that was available when I first went there. I was becoming increasingly distressed, because it was getting closer to the time I needed to move them and I didn't have a place for May. I was mostly doing this move alone; family and friends were working or otherwise busy. I would have to hire a mover to help me. Wallace had always been by my side to help, but he was out of the game now.

Meanwhile, I was going from the east side of Detroit to the north of Detroit visiting Aunt Helen, May, and Mom. Between those visits, Barbara and I were attending each of Wallace's doctors' appointments. After all the tests results came back it was time to hear what the doctor had to say. It was not good. A lump crept up in my throat, and I was trying not to cry in front of Wallace. I stepped out of the room to compose myself. When I got back in the room, Wallace received a telephone call and left the room. Barbara and I took that opportunity to ask the doctor his best guess at how long he had, and he told us maybe another year. Barbara and I were reeling. After we left the doctor, we consoled each other, and I tried to push away thoughts of not having Wallace around by continuing my search for a home for May.

After looking for homes again and not coming up with anything I could afford for May, I went to Mom's tired. I felt assaulted mentally and physically from this search and the news about Wallace. I decided to take a day off and go to my favorite spot on Belle Isle and find some peace in meditation. But I didn't. I had too many things on my mind. I thought to myself, *I need to see what's happening with the VA claim I filed. It's July now, and time is flying.* I had their number programmed in my cell phone, so I called the VA and spoke to a representative. He told me that they were just now processing applications from July 2010. I was not expecting that. Oh my God, what else can I do to get them to expedite this woman's claim? He explained she would have to demonstrate a "hardship" in order to move her claim ahead of all the others before her. Hardship meant that she had received an eviction notice, was completely broke and couldn't pay her bills, or was terminally ill.

Well, this put May in a catch-22, because she was not in any of those categories at this stage of the game. I was at a loss. I needed to have a plan B, but what that was going to be, at this point, I didn't have a clue.

A few days later, Mr. Haynes, the owner of Autumn Ravines, where Mom was moving to, called to tell me that a semiprivate room was available. This was wonderful news! I didn't hesitate; I told him I would take it. I began right away to downsize and move some of their belongings from the assisted-living home back to Mom's house. In the new home, Mom would have a room to herself and May would be sharing a room with someone else. So I only needed to take essentials and their pictures. I could feel the pressure and stress building inside me to get this move done.

One day, after I had loaded my rental car and was heading for my mother's house, I decided I needed to eat something, so I pulled into a McDonald's drive-through and ordered a couple of chicken wraps and a sweet tea. The young woman at the pickup window informed me that it would be just a few more minutes before my order was ready and asked me to pull aside. I pulled into a parking space and waited another five or so minutes and then decided to go in to see if they had forgotten I was outside waiting for my order. When I went in, they gave me my order and I left to return to my car.

As I was walking to the car, I noticed that something about the car was different, but I could not discern right away what it was. When I got to the car, I got in to eat my food and tried to shake off the feeling that something was wrong. In the middle of biting into my wrap, I put it down and got out of the car again. I returned to the back of the car and lo and behold discovered that the damn license plate was missing!

Okay. I thought, *No problem. It must have fallen off on these rough streets.* But something said check the front. Oh no. Rough streets didn't make both of them fall off; they'd been stolen! Seriously?! I couldn't even get mad; I was too damn tired. This was just another example of when it rains, it pours, and it was a given that things like this happen in Detroit. I was just very grateful that they didn't take the whole car!

I thanked God for that, took a deep breath, got back in the car, finished my wrap, drank my sweet tea, and headed straight to the police precinct. I filed my report and continued on my way home. The last thing I needed was for some cop to pull me over and have me jacked up on the curb assuming the position. Nope, wasn't trying to hear that, so I had my police report in hand as I continued on my way to Mom's house. When I got there, the same parking space I had parked in the night before was empty. So I pulled right into that space and got out of the car to begin unloading the boxes I had in the back. As I was doing that, I stepped on something. I looked down and saw that there were bolts on the ground. They looked like they could be the bolts from the license plates. I went to the front of the car, and sure enough, there were more bolts on the ground from the front plate.

But it got better. The kick in the head came from finding the butcher knife they must have used in the grass beside where the car had been parked! Damn, all I could do was laugh. People, what! I went in the house, told Barbara and Wallace my story, unloaded the boxes, called the rental car company to inform them that I was returning their car and why, and headed to the airport with Barbara along for company—as if I didn't already have enough to do.

A few days later, Barbara, Winnye, and I moved Mom's and May's belongings to their new residence. Autumn Ravines was very nice.

It had four bedrooms and large living spaces and accommodated six residents. I think this was just right; the small number of residents would hopefully allow them to get more individualized attention, something May complained about not getting at the larger assisted-living home (which housed ninety-one residents).

Once again, I waited a few days after moving them in to give them a chance to acclimate. A few days later, I began visiting. Mom was her usual cheerful self, and May was still the resident sourpuss. After being in Detroit for two months. I left for home. I was tired and wanted to see my husband. After I arrived home; my husband insisted we take a mini vacation in our RV to enjoy a few leisurely days together. Taking those few days for myself to decompress and get back in my home groove was exactly what I needed.

The second accounting was submitted to the judge in July, but his decision to approve it was postponed for proof of service to everyone listed on the report. Now my attorney had to send notices to May and the bond company. This postponement meant the hearing date had to be rescheduled.

In November, I received a letter from our attorney telling me that a new hearing was scheduled for January 23, 2012. Damn! By this time, May's money was running very low. I wrote letters to the court's attorney and our attorney, informing them that I had not heard from the VA on their decision regarding the application I submitted and I could not pay them until I did. In the letter to my attorney, I told her that I no longer required her services and that I would represent myself at the hearing in January.

I also told her that I was very disappointed in her for not being forthcoming with the information I requested from her in September, and now my trust in her had been compromised. When I sold the house the previous April, she had charged a whopping $1,500 fee that was taken out of the funds at close of escrow. When I questioned her about what services she provided for that fee, she evaded answering me.

She sent the escrow company a letter with instructions to take her fee from the escrow. I was cc'd on the letter (like I was an afterthought). I called her then and asked her why a letter didn't come to me first or a phone call or something informing me of her fee, and where was the invoice outlining her services? She explained that sending the escrow company a letter was standard practice.

Do I look like I have "stupid" on my forehead? What about me, the client? And her answer didn't address my question either. She was worried about getting her money; nothing more. I said this before: sometimes I think some attorneys and doctors think they can talk down to you and treat you any way they want to. Well, I'm not the average bear, and I push back when I feel I need to. I thought I knew the reason she didn't provide the invoice or advise me first—because she didn't like haggling with me regarding her fee. And at this point, I had no record of what services she provided to earn her fee. Hell, I was trying to save every bit of money I could where I could, and trust me, if I didn't ask I wouldn't know if something was possible or not.

In the past, when I asked if she could do better on her fee, she actually agreed to lower her fee a couple of times. After all, I was a client with three women who had money and assets, and we had used this attorney for every transaction to date over the past nine years. I thought that deserved a break. These women were not rich, and every little bit helped. We e-mailed each other on this subject in September, and she promised to provide me with the information. Now it was November, and I still didn't have it. I had been asking about this charge since last April. I would certainly get this information one way or another. She had known me long enough to know how tenacious I could be. At this point, after this long, I felt like she was hiding something from me.

There had been no correspondence from the VA regarding their decision to approve May for spousal benefits, and it had been a year since I submitted the application last November. Government agencies may exchange information. The VA insisted that May had been married more than once, and I had to prove to them that she was only married one time, to the same man for fifty-five years. I went back to the Social Security Administration and requested more information about the name change they showed on record. I was told that there was no other information besides the name. They could not tell me the first name of the husband or a date of marriage. Without this information I could not request a marriage certificate. So I obtained the information a different way. I contacted the State of Michigan Vital Records Department and requested a search for a divorce record between May and her known husband; there was none.

I believed the VA's slow response stemmed from the Social Security Administration showing this name change for May in June 1960. The second problem came about when I noticed that the information on her husband's death certificate in the maiden name section was entered incorrectly; it listed her mother's married name. The lesson here is to periodically check the information that is held by various agencies such as the Social Security Administration and credit reporting companies to verify that it is correct. Identity theft is very common these days, and it doesn't hurt to check on it.

Meanwhile, I needed May to sign a *Declaration of Status of Dependents* (Form 21-686c), declaring that she only had the one marriage. Oh God, just shoot me now. Getting her to sign papers was a chore. In early December, I sent the form to my friend Joann, who had been visiting Mom and May every week and checking to make sure they are being well cared for. Joann tried to get May to sign the form, and May refused to do it. She acted ugly, cursing and throwing Joann's phone and telling me in one breath that she would sign and then refusing to do so. I was livid. This benefit was for her, and if she didn't sign the form so I could get it approved, she would be homeless! I told Joann to just walk away and try again in a day or so. A week or so later, May signed the VA form, and along with some documents from the attorney, Joann mailed the papers. When I received the envelope, it was empty! The outer envelope was sealed! Nothing was in the envelope but another empty envelope that the attorney's papers had been in!

I called Joann and told her what I received. She insisted that she had mailed it and couldn't figure out what happened either. After I pulled myself together, I went to the post office and sent her more forms and a postage-paid Express Mail envelope (to return the form in). She got everything the next day and went over to the house to attempt to get May to sign the form. May refused—flat-out refused! In her defense, after the Nikki fiasco, I instilled in her not to sign anything anyone gave her to sign unless I said it was okay. But I was on the phone telling her it was okay to sign and explained to her what she was signing, and she still wouldn't sign. By this time, I was so upset, I was in tears! I thought, *I don't need this stress.* Again, I told Joann to walk away. A few days later, I enlisted the help of Mr. Haynes, the owner of the home, and he was able to get her to sign the form. I figured that the dominant male presence would help, and it did.

Joann sent the forms in the Express Mail envelope that Friday and I received it the next day, which was Christmas Eve. My husband came in the house about fifteen minutes after the Express envelope was delivered with our normal mail, and the first VA form that got lost was in the mail delivery!

What the hell is this, some kind of sick joke? No, the post office sent a letter saying that their equipment had torn the envelope and this document was found loose. I'd say Murphy's Law was alive and well. This really is real life. I couldn't make this stuff up if I tried. I immediately assembled everything I had waiting for this one document and headed to the post office. I sent the package of documents (signature required) on Christmas Eve. The VA received them in their office on December 29.

After all the trials and tribulations I had been through this year, I decided that I didn't want to talk about May, the VA, or anything else. I just wanted to enjoy my husband and ring in the New Year on a positive note. Darryl and I had a quiet evening watching the fireworks from our bedroom window and counting down the ball drop while we ate cheesecake and drank champagne.

# Chapter Five—Golden Sunsets and Doves

## 2012

### Aunt Helen

It was the New Year, and with it came renewed hope. I decided to call the VA to follow up and make sure that the package I sent was being reviewed by someone. I was always prepared to wait on hold when calling the VA.

Whenever I dealt with an organization, attorney, or doctor, I kept paper and pen handy to take notes. I included vital information, date, time of call, who I spoke with, and what I spoke about. This information can prove to be invaluable later on if I ever need it. The call center representative asked me if I had sent in the *Declaration of Dependents* document. I told her I did and it was included in a package of information that I sent and they received in their St. Paul, Minnesota, office on December 29.

She told me that she really couldn't help me until the documents had been scanned into the system and that would take three weeks!

I thought my head would explode! This was the fifth day of January, and that meant the end of the month. May was out of savings, and I had used her savings to supplement her pension and social security checks to pay for her rent and medication! Hey! Why was I surprised? Nothing—and I do mean *not one thing*—had been easy about this process! I had spent more time and energy on this application process than I had on all the other golden girls' stuff put together. In addition to all the VA mess, I had to get back to Detroit and attend a court hearing for the fiduciary accounting, which could not be finalized last year.

On January 20 I received a call from the court-appointed attorney reminding me that the hearing for the second fiduciary accounting was set for Monday, January 23. I told him that I would be there representing myself. In the matter of his bill, he informed me that he could not wait for the VA to approve May's claim and that he wanted his money now or he would put a lien on my bond (valued at $20,000), and I would have to deal with the bond company. He said he was tired of doing pro bono (free) work, and he had a staff to pay. He told me he didn't mind helping me as he had already given me a break on his fee, but he could not wait for his money. I explained to him that I understood and that I would pay him and reimburse myself when the VA claim was paid.

After his phone call, I continued to get ready for my trip. Later that afternoon while I was in the store, my telephone was ringing off the hook. Before I could answer the call it stopped ringing, and another call came right behind that one. When I answered the second call, the caller identified herself as a doctor from Sinai Grace Hospital. She said that Aunt Helen had been admitted and was in dire health. I needed some clarity! I asked her, "Are you telling me my aunt is dying?"

She said, "Yes. It doesn't look good."

My heart dropped, and tears began to burn my eyes. I ran out of the store to my car to hear what she was saying better. She told me, "Your aunt's blood pressure is so low that it is not pumping enough blood to her organs and there is no oxygen getting into her system. Her condition is deteriorating, and it is her time to go." She asked me if I wanted her to be put on life support. I explained to her that Aunt Helen had a do not resuscitate (DNR) order on file.

She assured me that on a ventilator Auntie would never have any quality of life, that she would be bedbound and suffer from bed sores. I agreed that was not what I wanted for her or anything that she would want for herself, since she had already signed a do not resuscitate (DNR) order. I asked the doctor to try to keep her alive until I got there. I was on my way and was leaving the next day at 6:00 a.m. She told me that she didn't think Aunt Helen would make it another twenty-four hours, but she promised that they would do everything to make her comfortable, and she would not suffer.

I thanked her and drove home and broke down and cried until I was dry. I wanted to be with her so I could hold her hand and whisper that I loved her. This was a stark reminder and déjà vu of Aunt Margaret's passing. I wasn't present when she died and neither was anyone else from our family, and I felt guilty then and now. I thought about a conversation I had at that time with my wise friend Winnye, who told me, "Cyn, even if you lived in the city, there is never going to be a guarantee that you would get there in time to be with any one of them; it would not make a difference when it's their time to go, but just know that Aunt Margaret knew you loved her." She said, "I lived fifteen minutes away from my mother, and I was not able to be with her either. You have done so much for your mother and aunts to show your love. You should not feel guilty about anything." She continued. "You have done more than most people would do, and I can't tell you enough about how proud I am of you. I am always amazed at how you take care of them and their business from across the country. Girl, they are lucky to have you."

I finished packing and lay down to try to sleep, but I could not stop thinking about Auntie. I eventually drifted off to sleep, and the phone startled me awake about 12:30 a.m. It was the same doctor telling me that my aunt was gone. I lost it again! The doctor was very kind and stayed on the phone with me the entire time it took for me to regain my composure. She also told me that there was someone with Aunt Helen the entire time. I was comforted some by this information. She asked if I wanted the minister to come in and administer last rites for Auntie, and I said yes and thanked her for her kindness and compassion.

When I hung up, I contacted the James H. Cole Home for Funerals and requested that her body be picked up. The young man I spoke with told me that I needed to sign a release first; then the hospital would release her body to them. I explained to him I was not in the city but was on my way and I would be there to sign it as soon as I got there.

My plane arrived that Saturday, at 2:45 p.m. and I was at the funeral home by 4:15 p.m. I signed the release and went to my mother's house. The first person I wanted to see was Wallace, to give him a hug and kiss. I was saddened to see his health was taking a turn for the worse, but he bravely continued to get up and get out of the house despite his discomfort.

My thoughts turned to my mom and how to present her with the news that her beloved sister was gone. I was torn whether to tell her at all, whether to take her to the funeral or just let it go, knowing that she would never really know. I decided to give it more thought as Auntie's death was still too fresh for me. One thing was for sure: I had things to do, and I did not have the luxury of self-pity. In addition to preparing for court on Monday, now I had a funeral to plan too. My daughter was on her way, and I felt comfort knowing she would be here soon.

By Sunday afternoon, I had spoken to the pastor at their church and had a confirmed time and date for the service. The pastor also announced Auntie's passing to the congregation.

I called family and friends and gave them the sad news and information about the service. Sunday night I only slept three hours. There was so much on my mind and so many things to do. I needed to focus and get my plan together. A habit I retained from working in the corporate world is to use a daily planner, which helped keep me organized. To avoid taking my planner with me everywhere I also used my cell phone's calendar, which has audible alerts; this is a very useful tool to have when multitasking.

Having already prepaid Auntie's funeral services was a huge help. My mother and her sisters and May and her husband had already paid for gravesites many years ago. All I had to do was take care of the funeral home. Now it was just a matter of picking out the casket, preparing the obituary, providing the funeral director with the outfit for Aunt Helen to wear, buying her undergarments, and choosing floral arrangements.

On Monday morning, red eyed, sleepy, and tired, I appeared in court to give the attorney his check and if necessary defend my accounting. Thankfully, it wasn't necessary. The GAL was instrumental in getting the report to balance this time; the judge signed off on the accounting, and that was done and behind me! The attorney assured me that he would help me with the next accounting; he said he could see that I was overwhelmed with responsibility. He gave me the website that attorneys use to pull forms needed for court. I explained to him that I still could not file the various petitions that might be needed because I lived out of state.

He told me not to worry and to send him the paperwork and he would review it to make sure it was correct and that I had the appropriate documentation to accompany it. Then he would refer me to another attorney who would file the petition for me for the filing fee and a small fee for their services. I thanked him, and we said good-bye.

After I left court, by the time I got to the house Monday evening, I had already completed the obituary, met with the church secretary, met with Ms. Cole, and picked out the casket and a two-piece suit for Auntie. I decided I wanted a few pictures to go on the obituary, so I sat down at the dining room table and looked through a number of photo albums, laughing and reminiscing along the way with my sister-in-law Barbara. In some ways, it was a painful reminder of all the family I had lost. But I decided as long as we had our memories they would never be forgotten. Now that court was over, I could give my undivided attention to making Aunt Helen's home-going first class.

Tuesday morning, I got up early to run errands and continued to the nursing home where Auntie spent the last seven years of her life. I thought the hospital had already informed the nursing home of Auntie's passing. It was a shock to me to find out they didn't know about her death, and it was a shock to the staff when I told them that Auntie had passed and I was there to gather her belongings. Everyone got quiet and gave me looks of disbelief, and then the tears started. One of the nurses buried her face in her hands and wept uncontrollably.

Others cried out too and embraced me. I became emotional again and was really fighting to keep it together so I could continue my day. Administrative staff members came to console me, and I expressed my appreciation to all of them for their kindness to my aunt. When I left there, I had her pictures and a coat from her room for my mother. I donated the rest of Aunt Helen's belongings to the nursing home for the homeless. I sat in my car, drained and trying not to cry, and remembered that I needed to call Debbie.

I said, "Deb, I am so tired and drained. I think I'll go to Belle Isle and sit by the water in front of the white fountain and try to decompress."

She said, "Of course you should go. You need to do something for yourself, Cynthia. Go on and take a break. Whatever else needs to be done can wait a minute." I stayed at Belle Isle for a while and began to feel some peace. I thought back over the years I had been taking care of my golden girls and all the things that had happened over those years and things that would continue to happen until they are all gone. I knew it was important for me to take care of myself, and I told myself that's exactly what I would do when this was over.

Now it was time for me to close Aunt Helen's chapter on Friday, January 27, 2012. I decided that I could not leave my mother out of the home-going for her sister, and even if she didn't remember, I thought it was appropriate for her to be present. My mom and her family had been members of their church for many years. They belonged to the choir, steward boards, and usher boards and were devoted members. I knew that there were people from the church who knew our family, and they would be looking to see Mom to express their condolences and to see how she was doing.

On Thursday, the funeral home completed dressing Aunt Helen and moved her into the chapel for me to view and make any changes if needed. I added her earrings to match the buttons on her suit—they had a little bling on them. I told her that she was going home in style in a way I thought would please her. We were alone in the chapel, and I sat down on a pew and wept. I told her how sorry I was that I was not with her when she passed. I wanted her to know she was loved, and I wanted her to know I did my best. I told her that we would miss her, and I asked her to forgive me. I sat there for hours waiting for others to come and view her, and no one came while I was there. After I got home, I reflected on why no one showed up that evening, and I realized that most of Auntie's contemporaries had passed, were home bound or in nursing homes, or were too afraid to come out in the dark and in bad winter weather.

Friday morning, the weather was cold and overcast; it really matched my feelings. Tonia and I were met at the church by my cousin and his family, Mom, and May. Mom and I were the first to walk down the aisle toward the casket. Once there, I asked Mom to say good-bye to her sister.

She looked at me and said, "That's my sister?"

I answered, "Yes, honey, it is. That's your sister Helen."

She stepped back as though she didn't know who Aunt Helen was. She probably didn't recognize her, because last year in August, I took her to visit Auntie and she said she didn't know who she was and recoiled from her and didn't want to kiss her. I believe that, in the Alzheimer's mind, the image she saw in her mind did not match the person she saw before her. Her current memory was steadily deteriorating, and it would eventually consume her past memories too.

When we sat down, Mom was surrounded by many people who came to pay their respects. The service was very nice, and the minister did a very good job of eulogizing Aunt Helen. The final words were said inside the Rosa Parks Chapel at the cemetery. Afterward, we proceeded to the entrance; there I released three white doves, representing her going home with her husband and her beloved father. Aunt Helen, rest in peace.

A lot had been done since I arrived a week ago, and every day I felt like I wasn't doing something I should be doing, like visiting Aunt Helen at the nursing home. I realized that there were those still living life who required my attention and my focus turned back to them. But no matter how hard I tried to jump-start my day, I was feeling sluggish. It seemed that I had run out of gas and hit a wall. I decided to take a day to grieve and rest. The Sunday after the funeral I stayed in bed and tried to sleep, but the phone kept ringing and visitors came by with cards and their condolences. As much as I wanted to, I couldn't stay in bed.

Wallace was constantly on my mind too, and I was concerned about him. I needed to talk with him some time before I left for home. We hadn't spent much time together because of all the other things I had to do, and he wasn't feeling well.

Monday I sat around the house quietly and tried to formulate a plan of action for what still lay ahead. A few days later, Wallace was feeling better, and I went downstairs to spend some time with him. We laughed and reminisced about things that happened over the years. Every time I was in town, we hung out at the movies, had dinner, and ran our errands together. He had been a tremendous supporter to me and played an important part in my mother's care. And it was because of him that she was able to stay in her home as long as she did. Without him, it would not have been possible. I loved Wallace like he was my brother.

Wallace and Mom were also very close. I was sure about one thing, and that is that my mother loved Wallace too. She would get mad at him and fuss about something he did or didn't do, but I could bet my last dollar that she was not going to allow anyone else to talk about her Wallace. Now he was fighting for his life, and it was hard to see him declining. I will say that Wallace was keeping his head up and staying as strong as he could. I could see in his face that the pain he endured was devastating and excruciating. I needed to get home so Darryl could come here and spend time with his brother.

Before I concluded my business and went home, I had to meet with Mr. Haynes at Autumn Ravines, pay May's rent for February and advise him about the dilemma I was having with the VA trying to get them to approve May's application.

I explained to him that I would have to find another home for her if they didn't give their approval soon, and per his procedures I was tendering my thirty-day notice to vacate. I told him that I would pay him for March with some of my own money if necessary, and he agreed to work with me with the hope that the answer would come before April's rent was due. With his assurance that we would work something out, I was comforted to know that I would not have to look for another home for her right now; I had been very concerned about that. At this point, I almost felt ready to conclude my business and return home.

But before I did, I turned my attention back to my attorney, who still had not responded to the messages I left with her secretary to call me. I wrote her a letter that essentially said that I would expect the information I had been requesting from her for almost a year by Friday, the tenth of February, or I would take another letter to the judge and request that he obtain the information from her.

Additionally, I told her that a similar letter would be mailed to the Michigan Bar Association Attorney Grievance Committee seeking their assistance, and I hand-delivered the letter to her office. I told her secretary that there was a time-sensitive letter inside and that I would strongly urge the attorney to respond before the deadline. I thanked her for all of her assistance over the years and then left. Two days after I delivered the letter, I had my information, in detail. Problem solved!

I elaborated on this situation to illustrate that staying focused on a problem can bring closure. I have found through past experiences that everyone has someone to answer to. I knew I could get recourse and how to get it. I also knew that she would not want the kind of trouble she would get if she did not respond this time. I don't expect to always come out successful, but at least putting out my best effort to right a wrong lets the other party know that I was not going to lie down and be walked on either.

After being in Detroit for three weeks, I had accomplished everything and more that I went there to do. I returned home on February 11. The minute I walked in the front door, I felt as though a weight lifted from my shoulders. But as in the past, that weight didn't stay gone for long.

On Monday, Darryl brought the mail in and called out to me that there was mail from the VA. I hurried downstairs and opened the letter. At last! They *finally* approved the claim for May's spousal benefits! I was so relieved that I felt as if another yoke had been lifted off my shoulders. Thank God!

But wait! I should know by now that another shoe had to drop. The VA sent yet another form that they needed May to sign! It was another statement of claim, but this time it was to waive due process for a competency hearing, since they had deemed May to be unable to handle her own affairs. Duh! Hadn't I been telling them this for a year now? And she must agree to me being her fiduciary. Here we go again! After all the trouble we went through to get the last form signed, I was not happy with trying to do it again.

Since Mr. Haynes was successful in getting May to sign the last form, I e-mailed him and solicited his assistance once again. He agreed to try, so I sent him the form overnight mail on Thursday and waited for the fireworks. On Sunday, (bless his heart) he did as promised. He attempted to attain May's signature. She cussed and huffed and called the man unflattering names. When he tried (unsuccessfully) to reason with her, she got worse. He called me and said, "Cynthia, I finally understand what you have been dealing with, and I feel bad for you. I had to walk around the house to get away from May, but wherever I went, she followed behind me, cussing and shaking her fists at me." He said, "She told me she had never seen me before, and she asked me who I was. I finally had to leave my own house, and that's never happened before!" We laughed about it, and he said that he would enlist the help of the house manager, Val, on Monday to see if she would be more successful. I thanked him and we hung up.

On Valentine's Day, I had an appointment to get my hair done. I was looking forward to catching up with my hairstylist, Kim. She had supported me through the years too. Kim really knew how to administer prayer with conviction, and those prayers had left me uplifted and hopeful. I enjoyed my visit with her, and of course, I left there with my hair looking fabulous.

I was at home enjoying the evening with my honey when my phone rang around 8:30 p.m. The second I saw the 248 area code come up on my display, my heart sunk. These late-night calls coming out of Detroit (it was 11:30 p.m. there) were rarely good news. It was Val at Autumn Ravines. She called to tell me that Mom had been transported by ambulance to the hospital. She said, "Cynthia, I don't want you to be alarmed. Your mom is not in dire health; it's just that I didn't think she was well enough for us to take care of her here at the house, and I felt she needed to be checked out."

Half an hour later, I called the hospital's ER to speak with the physician or a nurse on duty to find out, if Mom's condition was life threatening, to ask what was wrong with her, and to give them pertinent information about her. Long-distance caregiving kicks things up ten more levels. I had to assume that they may not have current information on her or her medical history records. I had to assume that they don't know that she had Alzheimer's and what stage she was in and that she would not be able to respond to them about most things coherently. At this point, Mom wasn't even telling the ER doctors her correct name. They were confused about who she was. (This is why I needed to talk with someone.) Mom gave them her maiden name, which was different from what they had on her record.

I'd say it had been about a year since she started using her maiden name. I remember the previous April when I was taking Mom shopping for some new bras. And as we were in the car driving along, Mom was doing her usual thing—being my copilot, reading all the street signs and billboards, and telling me when to go and stop—and I was asking her questions about family when she suddenly stated her name.

I said, "No, honey, that's your maiden name, not your married name."

In a very defiant voice she said to me, "I was not married. I know what my name is!"

And I asked her, "Mom, do you remember you were married to my daddy?" She looked at me with a blank stare. I said, "Come on, Mom. Tell me, who is my daddy?"

She quickly said, "Harry!"

I laughed and said, "No, try again. Harry was your brother."

Then she said, "Freddy!"

I said, "Mom, he was your brother too. You don't remember who my daddy is?"

She turned to me and said with a lot of sass, "I guess I don't!"

I laughed and told her, "Girl, you got jokes; I'm not an illegitimate child." Then I asked her again, "Do you know who my daddy is?"

Again, she looked at me curiously and said, "Maybe. Is he the guy who came by the house sometimes?"

Well now, at this point, I was in stitches, because she was totally oblivious to whom my dad was, and I just couldn't bring myself to continue that conversation; I gave her a big kiss and we went on with our day. It is so very hard to see them slipping away from you, and there is nothing you can do to stop it. Slow it down, maybe, but stopping was not in the cards at this point.

The ER nurse's voice coming on the phone line snapped me back from my reverie, and I gave her all the pertinent information they would need to try to get to the bottom of what was wrong with Mom; I hung up and called them back an hour later. I was told that she had pneumonia in her right lung, a bladder infection, and low potassium levels. Mom was admitted to the hospital so they could treat her, and I was able to rest a little easier.

The first day after Mom left the house, I called May, and she asked me when I was coming to get her. I said, "Coming to get you for what?"

"Well, you came and got Alice and just left me!" she yelled angrily.

I explained to her that Mom was in the hospital, and she asked me what was wrong with her. When I told her, she said, "You're a damn liar. I don't believe you!" and hung up on me. I called the next day, and when the caregiver told her I was on the telephone, she refused to speak with me. Man, that girl had some serious attitude.

Because Mom was in a strange environment and her routine was off, I assumed that she was not sure of what she was supposed to do. Her lunch tray was brought in one afternoon, and it sat on the table and Mom didn't touch it. The tray was still there untouched when Winnye got there that evening. She assumed that it was a dinner tray, but after she had the nurse heat the food and was feeding Mom, the dinner tray came in. When I found out about this incident, I was on the phone again to let the nurse know that Mom needed to be monitored at meal time. Every pair of eyes is helpful when your loved ones are not with you and you have entrusted them to the care of someone else. It was important to me that my friends and family were looking in on Mom and May. Joann and my cousin Darlene (who came into the picture after Aunt Helen's funeral) had been visiting the golden girls at the home every week, and I was grateful to them.

Mom left the hospital and went back to the house Friday morning. Later that night, my telephone rang, and when I checked the caller ID, I saw the 248 area code again and my heart skipped a beat. Once again, it was Val calling to tell me that she had Mom transported back to the hospital! She said, "Cynthia, I wanted you to know that your mom is not eating or drinking water, and although her condition does not seem any worse, it certainly is not better. I think she was released too soon." So the routine began over with calls to the hospital and so forth. Mom stayed in the hospital another four days. I was relieved when she went back to her familiar surroundings and her caregivers could work on getting her back into her routine.

Two weeks earlier, the VA had notified me that May was approved for her spousal benefit and she was finally getting her monthly checks. I was told that the next step was that the VA fiduciary unit had to contact me regarding how to be a VA fiduciary for them, and they would decide if I was qualified to handle May's money. Well, I had to think about that, and I asked myself, *If they were going to make the decision, then why did they make me go through hell to get her to tell them she wanted me to be the fiduciary?* When they called me, my first question would be whether I could reimburse myself for the out-of-pocket expenses I incurred for plane fare to go to court, rental car expenses, and payment to the court attorney. These expenses add up, and I certainly don't want to be financially impacted trying to help someone else when I have a household to think about too.

Conservators shouldn't have to use their money. We are supposed to use the protected person's money when they have it. In this case, I had to do something, and now I was hoping I wouldn't be penalized for helping her out. It took eighteen long months of dealing with the VA to get May's spousal benefits approved. And it was one headache after another that made me just want to scream. The bureaucracy was monumental, and repetitive requests for duplicate information were outlandish. I hope I never have to go through that again. But for all the nonsense I went through to get May this money, now that she was getting it, it was worth it.

## Wallace

With May finally getting her check from the VA, that drama had settled down, but I was still waiting for them to call me. I had the house to myself, because Darryl left for Detroit to spend time with Wallace and to handle his brother's business. We knew that Wallace's time was getting shorter, and we were living on pins and needles, jumping each time the phone rang. With Darryl gone, I turned my attention to me.

For me, exercising is good for my soul and body. Walking a couple of miles (or more) a day really boosted my spirits. Staying on course (without my husband's distracting food choices) and eating the right foods inspired me to keep working out, knowing that eventually the weight would drop off.

Darryl returned home in late March, and we continued our daily routines to keep thoughts of Wallace and his dire health situation from overcoming us. About 5:30 a.m. on the morning of May 1, 2012, I woke up suddenly and discovered that Darryl was not in bed. I could see the light from the television down the hall. I went to the bathroom and returned to bed. The phone rang, and my heart seemed to skip beats. After what seemed like an eternity but was only a few minutes later, Darryl came to the bedroom and said, "Honey, that was Barbara, Wallace is gone. He died an hour ago."

I responded, "I know. I woke up with him on my mind and was thinking about him when the phone rang."

That day, my husband made reservations for our trip home to bury his brother and my friend. He left a few days before me, and I arrived in Detroit a couple of days later. Services were held for Wallace on a Wednesday. I wrote a poem for him called "Let's Roll" that I read at the service; much to my surprise, the people laughed and gave me a round of applause for how well the poem depicted Wallace's personality.

No more suffering, no more pain, Wallace. Rest in peace.

## Mom

I remained in Detroit after Darryl left to begin cleaning up and preparing the flat that Wallace had lived in since 2008 for rent. While there, I took the opportunity to spend more time with Mom and May. Each day I went to the house to take them out for a ride. May refused to go, but Mom was ready, willing, and able. She still loved reading the billboards and traffic signs to me and giving me instructions on when to stop and go. We listened to music on the radio and sang. On one particular outing, Mom seemed to be in pretty good contact, so I decided to tell her about Wallace.

I said, "Mom, do you remember Wallace?"

After being quiet for a moment, giving my question some thought, she responded, "Oh yes. He's a nice guy."

I said, "I'm sorry to tell you, Mom, but Wallace passed a couple of weeks ago."

She remained quiet for a while, and I thought that perhaps she didn't understand me. But a short time later, she said, "Cyn, is Wallace really dead?"

I responded, "Yes, honey, he is."

To which she responded, "He was a good guy. I liked him a lot, and I will miss him."

I thought to myself, *Well, this was a good reaction,* and I continued to think about other things I wanted to tell her and ask her while she was lucid. So I asked her, "Mom, are you upset with me because I live in California and I'm not here with you every day?"

She turned to me and said, "Oh, Cyn, I could never be mad at you. You're my daughter. I appreciate everything you've done for me, and I love you."

If I could have pulled the car over and parked, I would have, because at that point my heart was so full I just wanted to sit and cry. I also felt a sense of relief. I admit that I had guilt feelings about leaving her, even though I knew that I was trying to honor her wishes. But with this revelation, I felt relieved. We continued our ride and stopped for ice cream before returning to the house.

This ritual went on daily. My childhood friend Belinda was with me one day when I went to get the ladies for their ride. As usual, May decided not to go out with us. So Belinda, Mom, and I headed out the door. While we were riding, talking, and having a good time, the song "My Girl" by the Temptations started playing on the radio. Mom, who was sitting in the front seat (so she could copilot), turned to me and said, "I know this song, Cyn."

I said to her, "Well, sing it for me, baby."

And much to my surprise my little eighty-four-year-old momma broke out singing at the top of her lungs. I turned to Belinda and said, "She really knows the words!" We joined Mom in singing, and we rocked it. We were so happy that day, laughing and singing. I'll never forget it.

The flat at Mom's house was rented, she was going to the center again and all my other business was concluded, so once again I headed back to California. I returned home in July and went back to my daily routine of calling my golden girls. Each day since I left, Mom asked me, "When are you coming? I'm right here waiting. Are you coming now?"

I would tell her, "I can't come right now, Momma, but I'll be there soon," and she said, "I'll be right here waiting for you."

I told Darryl, "Oh, I think I started something. Mom's waiting and looking for me to come and take her for a ride every day, and I feel bad that I can't." After a couple of weeks of this conversation, she finally gave up and didn't mention it any more. Even so, I had a subdued feeling that I couldn't shake. I was tempted to go back to see her, but I hadn't been home long, and I really wanted to spend time at home with my husband and recover from all that had happened while I was there.

On August 6, I received a phone call from Ms. Parker at the center. She called to tell me that she had some concerns. She said, "Cynthia, how often is Alice bathed?" I explained that she received a bath daily and was washed up before bed. I asked why she was asking and said, "Is there something wrong?"

She explained that she thought that Mom had an odor on her, but upon examining her, she was fine. I asked if she had ever smelled the odor before that day. She said no, but she would continue to monitor her on each visit. She also told me, "I want you to know, too, that Alice is not feeding herself and she's not pretending like she can't do it. We have to assist her, and she's lost a lot of weight." I asked if her concerns were such that I needed to return. She said no, she would keep an eye on her. I told her I would talk to the home manager to see if Mom was actually feeding herself there or if she required assistance.

At her age, and with her Alzheimer's getting worse, I felt that Mom needed more time to readjust to being back in the home after her hospital stay in February. I knew that she had lost weight too, but the caregivers assured me that she was eating well and showing progress in gaining some weight. I thought, *She'll bounce back, but it's going to take more time.* I knew that weight loss and loss of appetite are normal with aging and are also signs of the last stage of Alzheimer's, so I wasn't overly concerned.

I suppressed my thoughts and called the caregiver that evening. She assured me that Mom had eaten very well and that she had eaten on her own, watched her favorite television programs, and as always was in very good spirits. I asked to speak with Mom. When she answered the phone, I quoted one of her favorite rhymes. "Hi, Momma, I called to tell you that I love you once, I love you twice, I love you next to Jesus Christ!" and she replied "That's right!"

Mom was known for always reciting a rhyme she called "Brown Sugah," so every day that we talked, I said it to her, since she no longer remembered the words. "I ain't good looking, and I ain't built for speed, but I got everything a good man needs. I didn't come here to stay. I came here to play, and I'm going to leave this world in an uproar someday, because my daddy owns a farm down in Argentina and they call me *Brown Sugah*!" She laughed, and I told her she would always be my brown sugar, and then I told her, "Mom, I love you very much, honey," and in a very strong clear voice, she said, "I know you do, Cyn. I love you too." We conversed a little longer about her day at the center, and then I blew kisses to her through the phone and said good night.

The next day I went to my hairstylist, Kim, to get my hair braided. The braiding took longer than I expected, and before I knew it, time had slipped away and it was too late to call Mom. Darryl and I had our dinner and retreated to our respective "caves" to watch television. At about 7:30 p.m. Darryl came downstairs holding his phone and sat down on the couch across from me. I couldn't tell at first because the room was dark, except for the light from the television, that he was crying. I got up from my chair, went to him, and put my arm around him, asking, "Honey, what's wrong! What's happened?"

He said to me, "Honey, Mother's dead!"

166

I couldn't believe what he was telling me. "What? This has to be a mistake!" At this point, he gave me his phone, and Val the house manager confirmed what my mind was trying not to process. I dropped the phone and screamed out, "Noooo, she can't be gone! I didn't get to talk to her today! Momma! Momma!" I sobbed uncontrollably, with Darryl trying to console me. But yes, it was true. My mother lay down and passed peacefully in her sleep on Tuesday, August 7, 2012.

Over the next few days, Val did her best to comfort me by recounting my mother's last day. She told me, "Cynthia, your mother was in very high spirits, just like always. She had her favorite breakfast of pancakes, ate everything on her plate, laughed at her television programs, and had a very good day." I was comforted knowing that Mom passed quickly and didn't suffer. She wasn't hooked up to machines in a hospital, she passed in a home environment, Darlene and Joann had been to see her that day, and she was surrounded by people who had over the past year come to know and care about her.

During the last months that I visited with Mom, I had listened to her talk to her dead relatives, especially her mother. She repeatedly asked her mother to come and get her. She continuously said she was ready to go. "Momma, I'm ready. Please come and get me." I didn't want to hear those words, but Mom had said on a number of occasions that she was lonesome for her brothers and sisters and she wanted to be with them. I guess Aunt Helen didn't want her to be here alone, and seven months after she died she came back for her baby sister with God's blessing.

I returned to Detroit for the third time in seven months (and exactly forty days after leaving), this time to bury my mother. I tried telling myself that I had already planned funeral services for Aunt Margaret and Aunt Helen and I knew what had to be done and I could do it. Ahhhh, but this one was different, very different. This was *Momma*!

There was a nice turnout at the church, Mom's friends, coworkers, caregivers, and my childhood friends and relatives had many good things to say about my mother. I received many compliments about how nice her service was and that she would be proud of her home-going. At the gravesite eight beautiful white doves were released, symbolizing my mother and her seven brothers and sisters coming to escort her home. After all was said and done, mourners gathered at Mom's house to recount their stories of her. We toasted her and laughed and celebrated the way she wanted us to. Many years ago she had picked out the poem for this very day. It is called "I'm Free," and the first sentence says "Don't grieve for me."

We laughed about the funeral procession making its way down the street that Mom lived on for fifty-five years. When the hearse paused in front of Mom's house, the porch light popped on! I made a comment, "Look, Mom either just went in or just came out of the house." We laughed and talked about the funeral car driver taking a wrong turn that took us thirty minutes out of the way to the cemetery. We all laughed when I said, "Well, this had to be Mom's way of getting in a long ride before she took her final resting place. You know how she loved to go for a ride." We talked about how surprised Mom was when my childhood friends and I revealed our teenage antics to her after we were grown and long gone. Overall, it was a good day.

I love you, Momma. Rest in peace.

The impact of everything slapped me in the face after friends and family left Mom's house. My mother was gone. I felt so alone and empty, knowing that I would never speak with her again, hold her, kiss her, and take care of her. Missing her overwhelmed me. It hit me that I spent my twenty-fifth wedding anniversary at the cemetery signing paperwork. I was so overcome with debilitating grief that I could not celebrate my sixty-fourth birthday the Monday after the funeral. Days later, I went to the house where Mom had lived. I entered her room, closed the door, lay down on the bed where she took her last breath and wept. I was numb. This was the third death in seven months that I had gone through. I still had not fully grieved for Aunt Helen when Wallace passed, and even though I knew he was going to pass, his death still hit me hard. As I reflected on Mom and Aunt Helen, it dawned on me that not only were they close in life, but they passed the same year within seven months of each other. They loved each other, and I loved them.

I knew that grief counselors were an option through my health insurance. I could talk to my pastor or seek out a grief support group by looking online, but I was able to convince myself that I didn't need that right then. I gave it some time to see if I could pull out of it on my own. My family and friends and my faith sustained me through this difficult time. My grief came in stages: *Guilt*—Did I do everything I could? I should have been with her. *Sorrow* that I could not hear her voice, hug and kiss her. *Relief* that she no longer suffered with Alzheimer's and that she was where she wanted to be. And now I had less responsibility. *Closure*—a work in progress.

I realized that there would be a lot of "firsts" to deal with when they come around: her birthday in September, the holidays, Mother's Day; you get the picture. My family and friends were doing their best to console me and offer their best advice on dealing with my loss, and I thanked them from the bottom of my heart. I had to trust that God did not make mistakes and time would heal all things.

I knew that all the quotes and sayings sounded good. But being in the moment, the very fresh moment of my grief, none of those words mattered. When I returned to California, there were no visitors coming to the house, and the phone was not ringing. Every day brought tears and more tears; they seemed to come at the drop of a hat. I sequestered myself in the house and stayed away from everyone for fear that I would break down the moment they looked at me. I was unable to take care of business. I learned that grieving is personal and each person has to find their way through it on their terms. I turned a corner when I decided to resume writing this book. I began to exercise again, I returned to karate practice, and in general I slowly got back into my life. Mom would want that, and I know it. She inspired me in many ways, and I am grateful to her for many things. This book is my tribute to her.

# Conclusion

And so my story goes …

I believe that a caregiver performs selfless acts of kindness that put others' needs before her own. Sometimes necessity throws you in to the position of caring for a loved one. But however you arrive at that juncture, there will be many things you need to know and will learn along the way.

My advice to caregivers is to take care of yourself first so you will have the strength needed to help someone else. Caregiving is not easy, and many caregivers pass before the person they are caring for. Alzheimer's has its stages, and you too will go through stages in changing the way you care for your loved one to match the changing circumstances. I wasn't always prepared to accept a new set of symptoms indicating the progression was getting worse. I had to dig deep and move forward with whatever came my way. I had no choice; there was no turning back or opting out for me. I had to be there for the long haul.

I have had some priceless moments and endured scary situations and countless sleepless nights since I became involved with my mother's, aunts', and cousin's struggles with Alzheimer's. I was overwhelmed by the amount of information I had to go through to just stay up on techniques that helped me navigate my way to helping them. I was always afraid that I had missed something vital that could help them, and I didn't know it. But I learned by doing, and all the research in the world does not trump hands-on, in-your-face experience.

Book knowledge is good, but don't forget to temper it with common sense. I honed my skills for quick thinking and taking action. I had to resolve situations more creatively due to where I lived. I asked myself if there were things I would do differently, and the answer is a resounding yes! I made mistakes, learned from them, and moved forward. No one is perfect, and mistakes are bound to be made, especially in uncharted waters. Embrace them, learn from them, and move on.

Don't be too proud or afraid to seek assistance when needed. I was fortunate to have family and friends to assist me in caring for my golden girls. Don't shun the advice and counsel of others who see what you cannot or don't want to see. Ask questions of anyone who is or will be involved with your loved one or has any impact on your ability to be a caregiver and keep asking questions until you have an understanding of what is happening or what needs to be done.

There will be times when you want to scream and you don't understand why *you* have to be the one doing all the work, and feelings of guilt for thinking that way may overcome you. When you have been up all night and are tired as hell, you may think, *How much longer will this go on? When will I have my freedom back to do what I want to when I want to?* Those thoughts are normal; go with it and move on. But if you find that you are not moving past them and they are exacerbated with each passing day, seek assistance from a professional psychologist, clergyman, or doctor. Dealing with an Alzheimer's patient is a lot of work, and I commend you for undertaking the role of a caregiver, no matter what the disability.

Cousin May is eighty-two years old and is the last one of my four golden girls. I will continue to see to her needs until she leaves me too. Some days she is very lucid and knows me; other days not so much. Some days she cusses me out and hangs up on me; other days she is subdued and kind. Alzheimer's has run rampant through my mother's side of the family. I have said it before: when I have forgotten where I put my keys, a streak of fear runs through my mind. But I refuse to let myself linger on those thoughts of, *Is it happening to me?* I won't claim it, and I won't live in fear of it. I'm just going to live!

Alzheimer's disease stole my mother from me too soon. Although I had her physical being to hug, kiss, and hold, it took her memories and destroyed her thought processes. I was blessed to have her in my life for sixty-three years. If I had to do it all over again, I wouldn't hesitate. I loved my mother dearly and I miss her terribly.

To date, there is no cure for Alzheimer's, and there are many organizations that are doing their best to raise awareness and funds to support research for a cure. I am more committed than ever to continue my part in bringing awareness to this fight. *Please*, join me and countless others in fighting for continued research and finding a cure for Alzheimer's disease.

Good luck. Be diligent and stay strong.

Cynthia Young

# Caregivers' Resources and Information

**Michigan** (These are organizations I found useful when conducting business in Michigan.)

Autumn Ravines Adult Foster Care (AFC)
26864 W. 9 Mile Rd.
Southfield, MI 48033
(248) 568-5774
Website: www.AutumnRavines.com (for online tour and video)

Binson's (home health-care supplies)
Call or check the website for a location near you.
(888) 246-7667
Website: www.binsons.com

Caregiver Support Groups (Check the Internet and your local listings.)

Coleman A. Young Municipal Center
Family Court Division and Wayne County Probate Court
2 Woodward Ave.
Detroit, MI 48226

Department of Human Services, State of Michigan Family Independence Agency (FIA)
(for various services: food assistance, medical assistance, state disability, etc.)
Check your local listings.

Detroit Area Agency on Aging
1333 Brewery Park Blvd., Suite 200
Detroit, MI 48207-4544
(313) 446-4444
Website: www.daaa1a.org

Also, contact your local Area Agency on Aging (AAA). They may have information on living options and government services. To locate your local AAA, go to their website: www.n4a.org

Diane Hiscke, RN, MSN, CMC
Serving Seniors Inc.
330 East St., Suite 1
Rochester, MI 48307
(877) 375-7364
Website: www.servingseniors.net

Elder Abuse Hotline (24 Hours)—Michigan
(800) 996-6228 or (800) 882-6006
Check the Internet for more information from Michigan Adult Protective Services.
*(In an emergency, call 911 or your local police.)*

Fitness Works
6525 Second Ave.
Detroit, MI 48202
(313) 972-4040

Herman Keifer Complex—Health Departments Vital Records
Division (for residents who were born in or died in Detroit *only*)
1151 Taylor St., Room 104B
Detroit, MI 48202
(313) 876-4049 or (313) 876-0417

James H. Cole Home for Funerals
(Main Chapel)
2624 W. Grand Blvd.
Detroit, MI 48208
(313) 873-0771

Prosecuting Attorney's Office—Elder Abuse Unit (Check your local
listings.)
1441 St. Antoine St.
Detroit, MI 48226
(313) 224-5758

QualiCare Nursing Home
695 E. Grand Blvd.
Detroit, MI 48207
(313) 925-6655

SAC Adult Day Care Inc.
14200 Puritan Ave.
Detroit, MI 48227
(313) 270-2773

State of Michigan Vital Records Office (for births and death certificates prior to 10/01/78)
PO Box 30721
Lansing, MI 48909
(517) 335-8666

United Way (for Southeastern Michigan) Dial 2-1-1 (offers twenty-four-hour-a-day assistance: food, utility and rent payments, health care, etc.)
Website: www.211.UnitedWaySEM.org

Wayne County Probate Court (forms for guardian/conservator and more)
Website: www.wcpc.us

Wayne County Department of Human Services Adult Medical Services (Medicaid/Medicare)
2000 W. Lafayette Blvd.
Detroit, MI 48218

Waltonwood Assisted Living Home
3750 W. 13 Mile Rd.
Royal Oak, MI 48073
(800) 239-1396
Website: www.waltonwood.com

**California—Elder Abuse Hotline (twenty-four hours)**

Los Angeles County: (877) 477-3646 or (877) 4-R-Seniors

Riverside County: (800) 491-7123 or (951) 358-6998
Website: www.CDSS.gov for other county telephone numbers

**National Organizations**

AARP Caregiving Resource Center
Website: www.aarp.org/caregivers

A Place for Mom
www.aplaceformom.com
(800) 368-7242

Alzheimer's Association
20300 Civic Center Dr., #100
Southfield, MI 48076
24/7 helpline (toll-free, call anytime day or night): 800-272-3900

Eldercare Locator (Search for services in your community.)
(800) 677-1116
Website: www.eldercare.gov

Equifax (Credit Reporting Agency) (Check your local listings.)

National Alliance for Caregiving—offers information and resources
Website: www.caregiving.org

PACE
Free for those who qualify for Medicaid; others pay a fee.

Phillips Life Alert (Monitored Alert System)
(800) 380-3111

Medic Alert Foundation—Medical ID Jewelry
2323 Colorado Ave.
Turlock, CA 95382
(888) 633-4298

Safe Return (Alzheimer's Association Program)
For information, call (888) 572-8566

Senior Corps—Sends out volunteers fifty years old or older to visit the elderly at home and provide companionship.

SNAP for Seniors—Search for senior facilities, memory-care services, and payment options.
Website: www.snapforseniors.com

Social Security Administration (Check your local directory for listings.)

TRW (Credit Reporting Agency) (Check your local listings.)

Trans Union Credit (Credit Reporting Agency) (Check your local listings.)

Nancy L. Mace, MA, and Peter V. Rabins, MD, MPH, *The 36-Hour Day*, 5th ed. (Baltimore: The Johns Hopkins University Press, 2011). (I recommend this book.)

Villages (nonprofit support networks). Check the website to see if there is a Village near you. Help the elderly stay in their homes. Volunteers assist with everyday tasks.
Website: www.vtvnetwork.org

Visiting Nurse Associations of America—find at-home help in your state.
Website: www.vnaa.org

Department of Veterans Affairs (VA) Regional Office (Check your local listings.)
(800) 829-4833
Website: www.va.gov/va.form (for forms), www.va.gov (home page)

Veterans Service Organizations (VSO) (Check your local listings.)

***Note:***

The above organizations are listed for reference purposes only, and no endorsement is intended.

Contact information provided was current at the time of this writing and may change over time.

Use of these organizations is at the sole discretion of the reader, and the author accepts no liability.

## Prepare the House

Strangers may need to come in and provide assistance. You want to make sure that there are no valuables or sensitive information exposed and accessible for someone to take or copy.

**Keys**—Who else has keys to the house? Can you trust them? If you have doubts, change the locks!

**Valuables**—Go through the house and remove them immediately! Take them home with you or get a safe-deposit box at the bank.

**Will or Power of Attorney (POA)**—Look for these important document(s) and secure them as well.

**Health Insurance/Medical/Medicare Part A or B cards**—Keep these cards in a safe place. Medicare cards contain Social Security numbers. This information may be needed when you speak to health-care professionals or insurance companies and when you need to complete applications for various benefits.

**Social Security Card(s)**—Secure this card in a safe place. If applicable, also check for a deceased spouse's information.

**Gather Bills**—Check to see that they are current and whether there are credit/outstanding balances.

**Change of Address**—Have all mail routed to you so you can monitor and pay bills. This can be done online, or obtain a form from your local post office.

**Purging Information**—Anything with an account number or personal information on it needs to be secured. Always use a cross-cut shredder to dispose of important documents.

**Receipts**—Keep receipts for anything and everything you purchase on behalf of your loved one. It can help in the event that someone contests what or how you are doing things. Keep everything in a large envelope for the year and categorize items so that it's easy to access. If you are a court-appointed conservator, you will need this information for your fiduciary accountings.

**Life Insurance Policies**—Treat these like money and secure them in a safe place. Information on the policy will be needed when applying for a death-claim benefit.

**Burial Information**—Look for documentation that indicates that there are prepaid funeral arrangements. Also check for a prepaid burial plot. When making arrangements, be sure to inquire about the vault and opening/closing of the grave. These things are not usually included with the burial-plot purchase.

**Military Papers**—Was a spouse in the military? He or she may be entitled to VA benefits or the spouse of the veteran may be entitled to spousal benefits to aid in their care. The VA will require this information.

**Tax Documents**—Were they filed? Does a check need to be deposited or written to pay taxes?

**Do you need assistance?**—Contact the hospital's social worker for sources in financial aid (if applicable) and nursing assistance or respite care facilities. What about getting them to appointments and rehab (if applicable)? When looking for assisted-living housing, be aware that different states may call these facilities by different names (e.g., in California they are called room and board facilities; in Michigan, adult foster-care homes).

Abuse may happen when people who work in these homes never see visitors and may think that there is no one who cares about them. You must be vocal about things you want or that your loved one needs. But at the same time you must temper your request with honey. Use the vinegar only when it's necessary. Keep your eyes open. Watch your loved one's body language; he or she may be trying to communicate with you that way.

When seeking assistance for in-home care, make sure to interview and get references for anyone coming into your home, and make sure they are bonded! Consider running background checks (the application they fill out for employment with you should have a clause that they sign allowing you permission to do the background check) before you hire anyone. Consider checking their references, visiting their current residence, and running a credit report. Check with the bonding company. Also check the social networks to see if they have adverse or offensive information posted there. All of these precautions are necessary for your peace of mind.

**Preparing the House—Cleaning Out the House**

Take inventory of the big-ticket items in the house—furniture, appliances, car(s), etc.—and by each item, indicate one of the letters below:
S—Sell
K—Keep
T—Trash
D—Donate

Make sure you check with your local waste-management company to find out about bulk pickup days in your community. If their dates don't coincide with yours, ask for the nearest drop-off sites.

Be prepared to rent a truck or enlist someone who has one.

Label boxes with the letters listed above and use them to put smaller items in, such as linens, kitchen items, bath items, clothing, etc.

Make sure anything you have designated to "keep" is put out of harm's way to make sure it is not inadvertently discarded.

You may want to consider having a yard sale, but also consider that it is a lot of work and whatever is not sold must be put away for the next day (if you decide to do it over a weekend or maybe several weekends). Also, some communities may have associations and you may need permission before you can have a yard/garage sale.

Make sure all important papers have been secured and old documents shredded with a cross-cut shredder.

## Preparing the House—Keepsakes

I treasure mementos given to me by family and friends. Over the years (as far back as the seventies), I have kept letters and cards that my mother, daughter, and aunts sent to me after I moved to California.

When I realized that my mother's descent into memory loss was a stone-cold reality, I gathered all her letters and cards and put them in a scrapbook so I could look back and see a record of her thoughts over time. Oh yes, I sometimes break down and cry when I read them, but I also get some chuckles out of them too. Bottom line: it's just another way for me to hold on to her as she slips away from me. My mother loved sending cards, and I have many. I keep one of them on my vanity so I can read it every day. It says, "This is more than just a card … It's a hug with a fold in the middle."

Find a way to hold on to the good memories you have had with your loved one. I don't think you will regret it.

## Conducting Business

The majority of business I had to conduct took place in Michigan; some of the organizations I interacted with were national organizations. Check with your state for their website addresses, toll-free phone numbers, and local branches. Use the Internet; it is an invaluable tool to have at your disposal.

Before conducting any business, I wrote my questions down prior to making a telephone call(s). It saved time and perhaps multiple calls. During a call with a company representative, I often started with one question or an explanation of what I was trying to do or what I needed, and sometimes I got other information I didn't know about that turned out to be very helpful.

I kept a telephone log of conversations with anyone I spoke to when conducting business. I included the name of the person(s) I spoke with, date, time, and the subject and content of the conversation, and I kept the log with the paperwork for future reference. I also had file folders for each organization I dealt with, and everything was kept in alphabetical order so it would be easy to find.

I was incredibly frustrated with the lack of customer service when trying to conduct business on behalf of someone else. I encountered many rude people, but for every one of those rude people there was one who was very helpful when I told my story of what I was going through.

If someone is rude to you, never be afraid to ask for his superior. Every level of management has one. Shake things up if you need to, because complaining may get you to the front of the line.

Employees at hospitals, doctors' offices, dentists' offices, insurance companies, and other like businesses that handle health information are governed by the Health Insurance Portability and Accountability Act of 1996 (HIPAA). In short, this means that they cannot give out information that breaches a patient's right to privacy. It is incumbent on a caregiver to provide them with the proper identification and documentation to get the information needed.

Banks, credit unions, and credit card companies, etc., have a right to be skeptical, because there are so many people that scam and mistreat the elderly. So be patient when they are asking for your credentials and they are telling you what their particular organization requires to give you the information you are requesting.

## Finances/Banking

Uncashed or stale, dated checks: If the allotted time to surrender a check has not passed, you may still be able to cash it. Date information is on the front of the check. If the date has passed, contact the company that issued the check and ask that it be reissued.

If you are the conservator or have your power of attorney, you will need to send this documentation along with other documents the company or banking institution may require.

If a substantial amount of time has passed, you may find that the company or bank issuing the check has forwarded the funds for that check to your state controller and they will have those funds in an "unclaimed property" account. You can go to the state website and request the appropriate form(s) to claim your property. Again, you will be required to provide information to support your claim.

Another suggestion is to not be in a hurry to close bank accounts after your loved one passes. I made the mistake of closing Aunt Margaret's credit union account about four months after she passed. Little did I know that checks would be sent to me in her name and I could no longer deposit or cash them.

I wrote to the company issuing the check(s) and provided them with a copy of her death certificate and my information, and they reissued the check in my name. Hospitals and insurance companies may need to issue refunds for overpayment of premiums, etc., so I suggest keeping the checking account open for at least a year.

Credit cards: You may also want to run a credit report to see what credit cards they have. This will give you a baseline from when you took over. Periodically, check to make sure no suspicious activity has occurred since you took over. Contact credit reporting companies (Equifax, Experian, and TransUnion) for instructions on what is required.

# Legal

Depending on your situation, some of these steps may not be necessary. Because I am an only child and my aunts and cousin had no children, I did not have to consult anyone else before making decisions on their behalf (except for the court). This may be an issue in the event there are other siblings or family members who may not agree with what you want to do, and they may stall or thwart the decisions you want to make.

**Conservator and/or Guardian**—You may not need or want to apply for either of these documents. They are not necessarily linked together; they can be independent of each other. When/if you apply for them, a court hearing will be held and a determination will be made by the judge. Once you are a court-appointed guardian and/or conservator, here are some things you may want to think about:

**Will or** (if there is no will) **Trust**—If your loved ones are of sound mind, consider having them write their will or a trust so they can appoint an executor and decide how they want their estate disbursed and who they want to get what, especially when big-ticket assets are involved (home, car, money in the bank).

**Durable Power of Attorney** (if applicable)—This will give you authority to conduct business on behalf of your loved one. But it can only be done if your loved one is of sound mind. It is only valid until his or her death.

**Durable Power of Health Care** (if applicable)—This document gives you authority to make decisions regarding your loved ones' health care in the event that they cannot. It allows you to make sure that their wishes are carried out if they cannot do so and to communicate with their health-care professionals.

**Advance Directive**—This addresses medical choices pertaining to their wishes regarding life-sustaining support in the event of life-threatening illness, accident, etc.

**Birth Certificate**—Date-of-birth information is often needed when completing applications for benefits and services, or when speaking to medical providers, insurance companies, etc.

**Death Certificate of Person (Spouse)**—This is needed for applications for services or benefits.

**Marriage Certificate**—This is needed for Department of Veterans Affairs (VA) spousal benefits applications, Social Security Administration, and other agencies or businesses.

**Quit Claim Deed** (real property)—Obtain this from the registrar of deeds office (in Michigan at the City County Building).

Attorneys can be a necessary evil, and their fees can be expensive. However, if you feel confident enough to file court documents and represent yourself at court hearings, do it and perhaps you can save the money you would have spent on attorney fees. I hired an attorney because I lived out of state and had no clue what to do and how to do it in the early years. Back then, I also didn't have time to figure it out.

After I had to release my attorney, I found out that court forms are available on the Internet. With ten years of seeing what the attorney did and actually having experienced attending the court hearings, I decided to try my hand at it. I also have been fortunate enough to have an attorney willing to assist me by reviewing my paperwork and finding a local attorney to file those documents at the courthouse for me for the filing fee(s) of the document and a nominal charge for their services.

You will also be responsible to provide the court annually with an accounting to prove what you have done with the money, so keeping receipts is essential. You may be able to file your own paperwork with the court and get a hearing date. At the hearing, the guardian ad litem (GAL) will submit their report of your paperwork and make a recommendation to the judge to continue, suspend, or remove your conservatorship.

If you do not have an attorney to represent you, you may represent yourself (in the state of Michigan's Wayne County Probate Court). Take the following steps to get started: Log on to the court's website (www.wcpc.us) and click on General Probate and print the following forms: *Account of Fiduciary* (pc584), *Petition to Allow Accounts* (pc585c), and *Proof of Service* (pc564). (Check with your local court for more information.)

Follow the instructions on each form. Prior to the court date, the GAL may be in touch with you to ask for explanations for any discrepancies in your report and give you a chance to make corrections if you are out of balance.

In Detroit, Michigan, I went to the Coleman A. Young Municipal Building at 2 Woodward Avenue, thirteenth floor. You may want to do this when you are ready to submit your report. (Check your local directory for court address information. Courts in other states may not follow this procedure.)

An analyst will sit with you to review your fiduciary report.

To save time and multiple trips, make sure you are prepared to show a canceled check or receipt for every category you have listed on your report (e.g., rent, clothing, food, utilities, prescriptions, tax preparer, etc.). Also take the appropriate bank statements for the annual accounting period (e.g., May 7, 2011, through May 6, 2012) to confirm deposits, withdrawals, and interest earned.

Make copies of everything before submitting your originals. After the analyst reviews your paperwork, you must file it with the clerk. A filing fee is required.

Once you pay your fee, you will be given a hearing reminder. (This shows your hearing date.) Again, remember to keep track of your expenses and all of your receipts (for copies, parking, gas, mileage, etc.) to reimburse yourself (if applicable) and for use in the next accounting when spending money from your incapacitated person's account.

You will also need to prove to the court that you have notified all interested parties (including the incapacitated individual) by serving them with copies of the annual report and the hearing date so they may attend to present their objections to you as a conservator or your accounting. If you do not have names and addresses of family members, you will need to put an ad in the *Detroit Legal News* three weeks prior to the hearing date. There is a cost for this service. If you do not live in Detroit, Michigan, check with the probate court in your area for information on their method of notification.

Conservators must be bonded. As long as the person you are representing has assets, your bond is held to cover those assets. As their assets are sold off, you may petition the court to allow you to reduce or eliminate your bond.

Social Security Administration (SSA): If you are appointed the representative payee for a person receiving a social security check, then you are responsible for how you spend their money (keep track of all your expenditures). The SSA also requires an annual report be filed with them online or in hard copy each year. You will receive a letter with the hard-copy report and instructions on how to access the online report should you choose to go that route. Be sure to keep copies (for your file) of everything you submit.

Department of Veterans Affairs (VA): Spousal benefits awarded by the VA also require an annual report.

To find out more about veteran benefits, request a book titled *Federal Benefits for Veterans, Dependents and Survivors* (the last edition I had was 2010) by the Department of Veterans Affairs (VA Pamphlet 80-10-01 P94663). This pamphlet gives valuable website and resource information for the veteran.

## Respite Care

Some assisted-living and retirement homes may provide accommodations for an overnight stay or longer. What this means to you is a chance to have time for yourself while your loved ones are receiving the round-the-clock care they need.

Some facilities may also offer a suite for you to stay in for a short period so you can be close to your loved ones while they transition into their new assisted-living home environment. Ask if there is a fee for this service.

# Photo Album

## Aunt Margaret
### 1929–2007

Aunt Helen
1920–2012

Alice, "Mom"
1927–2012

Cousin Florence, "May"ola
1930–

# About the Author

**Photograph by Darryl Young**
**Hairstyle by Kim Best**

Cynthia Young was born and raised in Detroit, Michigan. She moved to California in 1974, where she resides today with her husband.

This is her first literary work. It was inspired by her experiences caring for four of her family members stricken with Alzheimer's disease.

She retired in 2005 after twenty-two years of service from her career in the aerospace industry as a human resources professional in order to expand her level of care to her mother, two aunts, and eldest cousin.

The journey with her golden girls began in 2002 and took place over the past ten years. Her story depicts the challenges associated with being a caregiver to her loved ones while living in California and commuting to Detroit to take care of them.